Introduction

This book started off as a critical analysis of the Barak Obama presidential campaign. As soon as I heard that Obama was running for the office of the U.S. presidency, I began to do research on who Obama was. My suspicions were that if the U.S. would allow an African {Black person} to even run for this "so-called highest office in the land", then the U.S. had sinister and nefarious intent. My research proved right - beyond any doubt! Deception was the order of the day as has been usual for U.S domestic and foreign policy! In doing the research, I was especially amazed at Obama's close working relationship with people who are without doubt, deeply involved in and with <u>the illuminati, an international force of demon worshiping empire builders</u> - a force of evil that, notwithstanding the myths and false accusations made about it, nevertheless, a realty in the realpolitik of past and current imperialism!

In doing the initial research and writing, I had no doubt that many of my people (Africans and in particular Africans in America {Black people} would hurl acid criticism towards me for analytically attacking the "anointed one"! But truth, like revolution, knows no sentimentality. I understood why many would think that the writing of," Obama Drama", was a betrayal to the cause and struggle of Africans in America; yet, I was also aware of the crisis of the colonized and oppressed. As Franz Fanon said in his classic book, <u>The Wretched of the Earth</u>, "The oppressed loved the ones they should hate and hate the ones they should love." On the other hand – a more truthful hand - I knew that only the truth would set us (African people) free and our people {Africans} and many other people, perished daily for lack of knowledge and critical analysis.

I do understand why many Africans in America voted for Obama; it was purely a reaction to the years of oppression and racism. It was an emotional reaction; it reflected the aspirations of millions of Black people. Many that voted had no prior knowledge of who Obama was, nor did they do any research on Obama's financial backers and right wing political supporters. For many people of color, their vote was a hope that conditions would change. <u>Africans in the U.S. voted out of aspirations and emotions not serious research and analysis</u>. This book offers a critical analysis.

The first edition {© 2012} was initiated during Obama's initial presidential campaign. The initial response of many, upon reading the first edition was critical and many questioned why the acid criticism and attack on the so-called anointed one. I knew quite early that the best reality to promote and support the book would be the realities of the Obama administration during its first four years and that the realities of the first and second term would provide empirical verification of the neo-liberal deception of the racist American ruling class and its willing puppet, Barak Obama.

Chapter One: describes the basis strategy of the Obama presidency, the financial backers of Obama and the intent of the U.S. ruling class along with the thesis of the book that Obama is a strategy of "RULING CLASS" deception. **Chapter two:** outlines the domestic strategy of the U.S. beginning in 2007. It has a recent update of the Obama administration and policy since he won the U.S. presidency. It exposes the class nature of Obama and race-class struggle in the U.S., the Zionist connection and influence in the Obama campaign and presidency along with the callous views and domestic policies of racist U.S. capitalism. **Chapter Three:** goes into much detail of the U.S. strategy for Africa and U.S. foreign policy. *Chapter Four and five are new chapters added to the book and comprise the essence of the second edition.* **Chapter four:** <u>*Betrayal: A Litany of Deception Lies and Hypocrisy*</u> deals with the contradictions of The Affordable Care Act and some of the major broken promises of the Obama administration. **Chapter Five:** <u>*State Sponsored Terror From Above and Below: Pawns of Azazyel*</u> concerns itself with drone murders of the innocent, U.S. sponsored terror and the growing American police State. **Chapter Six:** Offers suggestions and a model for solutions and corrective positive action

Chapter One

OBAMA DRAMA
STRATEGY OF DECEPTION – NEO-COLONIAL INTRIGUE

The African freedom fighter and philosopher June Bug Jabbo Jones would often say that Mr. say ain't nothing; Mr. do is the man. While Barak Obama undoubtedly is the dream, pride, hope and best candidate choice of millions of Africans in America and also the hope or at least the shrewd choice of many White Americans and a significant sector of the U.S. capitalist ruling class and racist right wing, there is much to be said that has not been said and much more to be revealed that has not been adequately revealed concerning this "great White hope!

In spite of Obama's populist rhetoric and even with his advocacy for change and pledges of alleviating deteriorating social conditions facing average Americans and promises of tax cuts for working people, health care reform, better pay and a government that would protect pensions, not CEO bonuses, Obama's unquestionable political allegiance to his ideological and financial sponsors exposes his charade of populist rhetoric and confirms the suspicions of many Africans in the U.S. – at least those not in confusion and denial. Obama's unquestionable political allegiance to his ideological and financial sponsors argues in a tenaciously and culturally embarrassing way for a person that has betrayed his people, prostituted his ethics, and a Franz Fanon points out in, *"Pitfalls of National Consciousness"* shows Obama to be a willing instrument of his people's own oppression.

My parents would often warn me that the company you keep is a good description of not only who you are but what you are. The adage birds of a feather flock together has meaning with Obama and in this reference he flies or is carried by political vultures and old eagles that now have very little places to roost or at least roost in safety. **The dying**

buzzard of U.S. imperialism needs a face lift, an image to fool the world, especially the African world. U.S. imperialism needs to create an image of change, a deception, needed to continue its ugly American program of world plunder and greed. Those who choose to fly with the U.S. will crash with it also! So Barak can further insult the ebony polished legacy of Dr. King with speeches of "our dream will not be deferred", "our future will not be denied", and "our time for change has come." But who is the "our" and what change is he referring to. Barak "ain't" with the masses and his change "ain't" what we are struggling for!

Obama's populist primary rhetoric was only one unsightly blemish of a face that stands before the flag of America and all the horror, oppression, exploitation, racism and two-facedness that it represents. He stands for and promotes and pledges to uphold the law, even if it supports cops who shoot tens of bullets into a Sean Bell.(2) even if the U.S. law betrays thousands of Africans in New Orleans, even if the law ignores a tragedy like Jena Six. There is another unsightly blemish on the face of Barak Obama and it is turned firmly towards the very corporate interests he publicly criticizes, which has poured tens of millions of dollars into his election campaigns. It is a face – even if a Black face – that says I will be the mouth piece for a forked tongue foreign policy and a mask that will seek to trick many in Africa into accepting U.S. strategy, U.S. military, U.S. intrigue, U.S. capitalism and U.S. neo-colonialism. How can you be for the little person and at the same time tenaciously being for the few that seek to live off the backs and misery of the mass of the people? As some would say in some communities, "we ain't falling for the dumb stuff!"

On the day after the Potomac primaries, *Business Week (the comic book of the ruling class)* ran a special report entitled, "Is Obama Good for Business?" The piece provided no direct answer to this question, but the attitude taken by the business magazine appeared to be a qualified "yes," based in large part on the private discussions that the Illinois senator is holding with top Wall Street and corporate insiders even as he is delivering his public appeals for "change" and comparing himself to

Dr. King. Remember it was Dr. King who got his head blow off for advocating a radical redistribution of economic wealth and power in the U.S. After learning of his victory in the Maine Democratic caucuses, Obama sat down at his computer to exchange emails with Robert Wolf, CEO of UBS America, one of his major Wall Street "bundlers," responsible for bringing in millions in donations from fellow multi-millionaires to finance what Obama referred to as his "movement." According to estimates made by the Center for Responsive Politics, <u>80 percent of the money raised by the Obama campaign last year came from donors affiliated with business, with Wall Street leading the pack.</u> More than half of the money came in the form of donations totaling $2,300 or more.

In addition to Wolf, Obama stays in regular touch with Warren Buffett, the second-wealthiest individual in America, with a net worth of some $52 billion. Among his leading economic advisors is Austan Goolsbee, a University of Chicago professor and prominent advocate of free market policies; in other words **Obama is backed, encouraged and financed by the worst of blood sucking capitalist**. Yet Obama out of his double-dealing and betraying mouth could say on the campaign trail such hypocrisy as: he is concerned with helping "the father who goes to work before dawn and then lies awake at night wondering how he's going to pay the bills" , or "the woman who told me she works the night shift after a full day at college and still can't afford health care for a sister who's ill;" or the retiree "who lost his pension when the company he gave his life to went bankrupt;" and "the teacher who works at Dunkin Donuts after school just to make ends meet." Obama is full of the most toxic type of U.S. capitalist garbage and vomits out of his mouth whatever his Zionist and capitalist bosses pour into his moral-less brain! As wrong as Hillary Clinton is, she was right on calling Obama elitist! Not only is he elitist. He is a dangerous subterfuge, a manikin polished by the best of media and Madison Avenue and most unfortunately for Africans in the U.S., **a regime puppet that will dash the hopes and aspirations of millions.** But such is the hard medicine needed to jar millions of Africans in the U.S. out of an addiction of denial and deception!

Obama: Class and Class Struggle

In Class Struggle in Africa, Kwame Nkrumah says: "Class struggle is a fundamental theme of recorded history. In every non-socialist society there are two main categories of class, the ruling class or classes, and the subject class or classes. The ruling class possesses the major instruments of economic production and distribution, and the means of establishing its political domination, **{including the U.S. presidency}** while the subject class serves the interests of the ruling class, and is politically, economically and socially dominated by it. There is conflict between the ruling class and the exploited class. The nature and cause of the conflict is influenced by the development of productive forces. That is, in any given class formation, whether it be feudalism, capitalism, or any other type of society, the institutions and ideas associated with it arise from the level of productive forces and the mode of production. The moment private ownership of the means of production appears, and capitalists start exploiting workers the capitalists become a bourgeois class, the exploited workers a working class. For in the final analysis, a class is nothing more than the sum total of individuals bound together by certain interests which as a class they try to preserve and protect."

Obama represents a sector or class of the Africans in the U.S. that are hell bent on supporting the multinational class headed by the American ruling class, and Obama represents a sector or class benefiting from world imperialism and American capitalism; in fact, he represents the upper sectors of the African bourgeoisie. **Be not confused by this term bourgeoisie! Especially for the African, it is neither best defined nor understood by just a simple analysis of income, type of car, wealth, neighborhood and dress.** Such items are not the best indicators of the self-centered and anti-mass views that this class holds as mandatory tenets of its elitist ideology. However, this is not to say that all who are a part of this class are dedicated to its values, as Amilcar Cabral very clearly states(3) Some in the African bourgeoisie class have consciously decided to commit class suicide. Bourgeoisie in - a negative sense - is an ideology where those individuals who are considered members of the elite see themselves as a select group of people with outstanding personal abilities, intellect, wealth, specialized training, experiences and - in regards to the African - a group that sees itself as having favor by the ruling class of America who will reward good Americans" **"good slaves"** for their blind allegiance. This African bourgeoisie class views the masses of African people with disgust and seeks to avoid any contact with them; they look down their noses so to speak on the mass as ghetto and will go out their way to make their disassociation and disgust with the mass of their people. They view the mass with contempt and at every chance disassociate themselves with mass concerns and relations and will go so far as to make it clear to the White bourgeoisie class and even the White working class, that they are a miles apart, " in every way" from the masses of African people. This is the kind of African that will promenade and boast that they are not Black - they are Americans. Some will even dare dress in African garb and attend ritual festivals, but their soul is in American capitalist values and their own reprobated greed and self-interest! They will support the cause of the U.S., even if it means turning a deft ear on the aspirations of the masses of Africans who – had it not been for the people's mass struggles - would not be in the positions of power and prestige that they currently occupy.

The following quotes by Kwame Nkrumah, from his *Class Struggle in Africa*, shows the significance of a class analysis for the African and reveals the uniqueness of this reality in terms of the African context.

"Each historical situation develops its own dynamics. The close links between class and race developed in Africa alongside capitalist exploitation. Slavery, the master-servant relationship, and cheap labor were basic to it. The classic example is South Africa, where Africans experienced a double exploitation -- both on the ground of color and of class. Similar conditions exist in the USA, the Caribbean, in Latin America, and in other parts of the world where the nature of the development of productive forces has resulted in a racist class structure..."

"While racist social structure is not inherent in the colonial situation, it is inseparable from capitalist economic development. For race is inextricably linked with class exploitation; in a racist-capitalist power structure, capitalist exploitation and race oppression are complementary... "

"In the modern world, the race struggle has become part of the class struggle..."

Obama is the race card now being played on a neo-colonial level. Obama represents a strategy that seeks to blur and hide the reality of class antagonisms (inside and outside of the African context) and the racist policy of a capitalist ideology and stratagem, but this is consistent with neo-colonialism which seeks to hide the real hand of power, a power that is quite content on manipulation from real sources of power behind the façade of a Black, media made smiling face!

Nkrumah warns and advises that:

"A determined attack must be made on the entrenched position of the minority reactionary elements amongst our own peoples. For the dramatic exposure in recent years of the nature and extent of the class struggle in Africa, through the succession of reactionary military coups and the outbreak of civil wars, particularly in West and Central Africa, has demonstrated the unity between the interests of neocolonialism and the indigenous bourgeoisie." {Ibid: Class Struggle in Africa}

American capitalism and world imperialism are in dire straits. American capitalism needs a new strategy to cope with the impending threat. A condition of permanent destabilization and drastic downturn is the order of the day for capitalism, the shrinkage of markets along with the scramble for sustainable resources, the political-military challenges, setbacks and defeats, the growing isolation of

American ideology coupled with the world demand for debt payment, the grave volatility of the U.S. dollar, the internal growing resistance and growing misery of millions of hurting people, and the inevitable growth of a fascist police state, are a testimony that things are going very wrong and very bad in the good old USA. A 911 desperation strategy was needed by the American ruling class. But Like 911, the Obama Drama will be exposed, soon and very soon!

Deception, even mass deception, has been a stratagem of empires for centuries. Couple this old technique with the disabling abilities of a mass media with technological acumen, along with a colonized, disorganized and self-centered mass, and you have a condition of guaranteed control and exploitation. Obama is a tool intent on deception, media-creation, false promises and contrived unconsciousness of the people. <u>Make the people think a change is coming, while you prepare for an offensive of domination and elimination.</u>

Although Obama makes sound bite references to the deteriorating conditions of working people - declining wages, rising medical costs, education and other living expenses, the shifting of jobs to low-wage countries - <u>this is not presented as the product of capitalism, and a social and economic system that benefits the wealthy at the expense of the working class.</u> Instead, Obama claimed, these conditions were the result of "lobbyists" in Washington who used their money and influence to crush good ideas and "politicians" who spend too much time trying to score political points instead of "trying to bridge their differences so we can get something done." In fact, Obama is only proposing to spend $6 billion a year on infrastructure repair – far less than the monthly cost of the war in Iraq - and an infinitesimal drop in the bucket compared to the $1.6 trillion the American Society of Engineers says is required to bring the nation's infrastructure up to good condition. Obama makes no mention of the 3.5 trillion that is pumped into the war arsenal for the U.S. occupation and invasion of Iraq or the over one trillion for the U.S. invasion of Afghanistan. Just the cost of one B-1 bomber ($200 million) could dramatically relieve the misery of a deteriorating domestic infrastructure, or improve the quality of education, food and housing in the poorest communities in the U.S. While Exxon makes 15,000 per second and brags of a third quarter net profit of over $9.92 billion, Obama speaks of a tax rebate of $1,000. With just the price of gas and bread this will not last but a few weeks and that is id one only buys bread and gas! While billions in the Katrina relief funds are missing, Obama, and those who dictate to him, are intentionally missing the need to provide for the "domestic tranquility." **Obama is a strategy of deception and a tool of the ruling class!**

OBAMA HAS THE ENDORSEMENT OF THE NEO-LIBERAL RIGHT WING

If politics makes strange bed fellows, then Obama has amassed a curious assemble of sleep around partners.

The Volcker endorsement

The endorsement of Obama by Paul Volcker, who was appointed Federal Reserve Board chairman by Democratic President Jimmy Carter in 1979 , and remained in charge of the U.S. central bank, the Federal Reserve - a Zionist instrument - for nearly seven years under the right-wing Republican administration of Ronald Reagan. Volcker (another instrument of the American ruling class) was responsible for inaugurating a high-interest-rate regime demanded by the dominant sections of finance capital in the name of the battle against inflation. Volcker's monetary policy was inextricably linked to the offensive against the masses of many cultures and was launched with the firing of the air traffic controllers and the breaking of the PATCO strike and continued with the shutdown of large sections of basic industry and the unleashing of the worst economic downturn since the Great Depression of the 1930s. The venom of capitalism again struck without prejudice to all people notwithstanding the fact that for people of color the poison was intentionally and systematically a huge racist overdose. The ultimate effect of these policies was a vast transfer of wealth from the mass of working people to narrow financial elite, a process that has continued to this day. Obama applauded the Volker endorsement as a sign of people approval, but what people are we speaking of and how few?

In a statement announcing his backing for Obama, Volcker noted that he had previously avoided involvement in partisan politics. He said that he was moved to intervene now not "by the current turmoil in markets," but because of "the breadth and depth of challenges that face our nation at home and abroad." He added, "Those challenges demand a new leadership and a fresh approach." Obama's leadership, he concluded, would be able to "restore needed confidence in our vision, our strength and our purposes right around the world." I say." **Obama is a strategy of deception!**

Larry Kudlow, the right-wing pundit and former Reagan administration economic advisor, commented on the endorsement noting that he had once worked as a speechwriter for Volcker and describing him as a great American... a classic conservative... a man of fiscal and monetary rectitude. Volcker, Kudlow wrote, would not have made this endorsement on a whim. Believe me. He never gets involved in these kinds of political decisions. He concluded by asking: Is Volcker the new Robert Rubin [the Wall Street insider who directed the Clinton administration's economic policy, a policy that was devastating to the poor, working class and the mass of Africans. Is it possible that Mr. Volcker is somehow tutoring Obama? Is it possible that Obama is more financially conservative than originally believed? **YOU DAM RIGHT HE IS!**

These are the real relations that are being forged behind the scenes as Obama delivers left phrases from the podium. <u>Those like Volcker see the Illinois senator as a useful vehicle for effecting major changes aimed not at ameliorating the conditions of life for masses of working people, but rather at securing the global interests of American finance capital. .</u>" **Obama is a strategy of deception!**

No doubt, the ruling class is gambling on that Obama, who would be America's first African-American president, is best suited to confront the dangers posed by continuing economic crisis and rising social tensions. Who better to persuade the masses not to rebel as they did in the turbulent sixties, who better to demand even greater sacrifices from the working class, all in the name of national unity and **"change?"** Who better to misinform and deceive Black people in Africa that that the "great White hope of America is a savior and humanitarian solver of African problems. At the same time, Obama would present a fresh face to the world, which the American ruling class hopes would help extricate U.S. imperialism from the foreign policy debacles and growing global isolation that is the legacy of the Bush administration, and a failing neo-liberal policy. Given his big business ties, Obama's campaign rhetoric about confronting poverty and social inequality involves a level of cynicism and demagogy that is truly staggering. His incessant promises of change are not tied to any radical economic program that fundamentally challenges the profit interests of the giant corporations and Wall Street and his media conspired comparisons to Dr. Martin Luther King, is culturally insulting and is as a-historical as Columbus discovering the western hemisphere!

On the contrary, and in ostentatious contradiction, Obama has advanced a neo-liberal fiscal policy, pledging himself to a "pay as you go" approach and stressing the need to reduce debt and deficits. Given that he would take office with a near-record $400 billion deficit inherited from the Bush administration, and a plummeting US dollar, coupled by shrinking international markets and a peak oil reality, it is clear, <u>or it should be clear</u> that the Obama domestic agenda - if he wins - will be one of extreme austerity measures, a growing and menacing police state, depression and a foreign policy locked into a strategy of attempted world plunder, desperation and increasing isolation, defeat and capitalist demise. **Obama is a strategy of deception!**

While a candidate touring a General Motors plant in Janesville, Wisconsin, Obama put forward a so-called jobs program involving investments in infrastructure and alternative energy that would total $210 billion over 10 years. In the face of the deep-going crisis confronting American capitalism, this is less than a drop in the bucket—

and even this drop would quickly evaporate in the face of demands for deficit reduction. To the Military Industrial Complex, Obama has promised increases to a US military budget—which consumes an estimated $700 billion annually!

Those who don't want to talk about capitalism should by rights keep their mouths shut when it comes to poverty and unemployment. One cannot seriously deal with either poverty or unemployment without confronting the private ownership of society's productive forces and the immense social inequality that it has created. The defense of jobs and living standards, the right to decent housing, health care and education for hundreds of millions of in America can be advanced only through a radical redistribution of wealth from the super-rich to the broad mass of working people. Clearly, the likes of Wolf, Buffett and Volcker are backing Obama because they know that he has no intention of going anywhere near such a policy.

It was millions in "startup money" from wealthy backers that made it possible for a very junior senator from Illinois, a man who four years ago was serving in the Illinois state legislature and unknown nationally, to become a viable presidential candidate. The largely flattering treatment of the Obama campaign, by not only the liberal sections of the media but in the right-wing press as well, reveals his class interest and support. Among those backing the Obama campaign are such pillars of the U.S. political establishment as Zbigniew Brzezinski, national security adviser to President Jimmy Carter and co-author of the notorious National Security Council Memorandum #46 and arch-Cold Warrior; retired Air Force General Merrill McPeak and a host of other retired military brass; billionaire, along with Warren Buffett, the second-richest man in America; and an array of Wall Street and corporate executives, none of whom could be suspected of any sympathy for radical social change. This Robber Barron assemble of selfishness and callous mass contemptible profiteers of doom, have never and will never have any sympathy or regards for the rights of the masses of the people. It is to this host of evils that Obama and Mitchell pledge their allegiance to. *Oh! I know what you are saying.* **If not Obama then who or what. Keep reading! I'm saving the desert till last!**

Obama is merely the product of an effective marketing campaign which has utilized media savvy and technology to sell this new version of a very old product - the Democratic Party "friend of the people," previously disgustingly incarnated in the "insurgent" candidacy of Jimmy Carter in 1976, then in the "man from Hope," Bill Clinton himself, in 1992. An Obama presidency would no more represent a fundamental change in American politics than the election of Carter and Clinton did, or the election of Lincoln, Roosevelt or Kennedy did and if the Obama presidency-hopeful did it would never be allowed anywhere near presidential campaign!

The Domestic Strategy

A *Look at conditions in 2011 and 2013*

The initial writing of this book began when Barak Obama first announced his intent to run for the office of the U.S. presidency in February 10, 2007. Most of the book was completed by the first few month of his presidency. The policies and events that have transpired since 2007 have confirmed much that was said in the initial writing of this book. But a few updates here only serve to make more concrete the essence of this book and that is clear proof that the Obama presidency is a strategy of the U.S. ruling class and an act of enormous deception.

Barack Obama's first months have been dominated by a global economic crisis, a continuing war in Iraq and an escalation of U.S. aggression in Afghanistan - continuing the militarist and aggressive thrust of the Bush administration's policies, a devastation of jobs along with health care and public education of a scale not seen since the Great Depression, and intervention in court cases to lock away as state secrets information about the massive government spying operation directed against the population. ***Obama's first 100 days have made clear the right-wing character of his administration and the class interests it serves.*** This can be seen in just highlighting a few topics relative to the Obama administration in 2011: the attack on workers, health care, domestic welfare, public education, and the invasion of Libya and Obama's disdain for his own people – the African!

ATTACK ON WORKERS- the *job crisis in America*

In 2011 working people in the U.S. experienced the worst mass unemployment since the depression years of the 1930s. States throughout America began making severe cuts in unemployment payments while bankers, CEOs and corporate profits flourished in downpours of wealth and luxuries. The vindictive and punitive measures which threaten millions of workers and poor families with destitution were led by the Obama administration and the ruling hand that guides it. President Obama dismissed concerns over the June 2011 disastrous jobs report during a joint White House press conference with German Chancellor Angela Merkel, another enemy of the people. The president suggested the figures—which showed an increase in the national jobless rate rising 9.0 to 9.1 percent in May of 2011 and that the average length of unemployment reaching a record high of nearly 40 weeks—were an anomaly. Actual unemployment figures for young people in the U.S. then was at staggering levels: 30% for all young people, 45% for young Latinos, and as high as 66% for African {Black} youth! Of course it is worse in 2014. In addition, the White House is engaged in ongoing talks with Republican leaders to gut long-standing entitlement programs like Medicare and Medicaid in order to pay for the Wall Street bailout and the extension of massive tax cuts to the rich.

In 2011, the administration's indifference to the plight of tens of millions of unemployed and underemployed workers provoked widespread anger against the president. A *Washington Post*-ABC News poll indicated that 59 percent of respondents gave Obama a negative rating for his handling of the economy. Eighty-nine percent of Americans say the economy was in bad shape; 57 percent said the recovery has not started and 66 percent said the U.S. was seriously on the wrong track. Overall, the president only had a 47 percent approval rating; in December of 2013, his rating was at 41% and falling rapidly

The administration showed callous indifference to the conditions of the mass: government austerity measures, the closure of schools, cuts to Medicare and Medicaid, and the layoff of hundreds of thousands of government employees on both the state and federal levels. The ultimate aim being to create conditions in which millions of people have no access to even the most basic government assistance, to create such levels of economic desperation that workers will take any job, at any wage. The talk of an "economic recovery," the jobs situation is disastrous. Eighteen states and the District of Columbia had official jobless rates of 9 percent or more in April of 2011, while real unemployment is much higher. There are currently 24 million people in the United States who either want to work but can't find it, or are working part-time involuntarily. This figure is larger than the populations of Chile or the Netherlands, and is twice the population of Cuba.

Currently {January of 2014}, some 5.8 million U.S. workers have been out of work for over 67 weeks or more. Economists estimate that one million people lost all federal unemployment benefits last year after being unable to find work for 99 weeks. Nearly two million people total are among this group of "99ers."." The U.S. employment report of June 2011 documented the horrendous reality of worsening conditions for workers and the unemployed. It showed that far from a recovery, the mass of people in America face a deepening crisis more destabilizing and destructive than the Great depression of the 1930s. This situation is part of a global deceleration of destabilization of the world capitalist system. The slowdown in manufacturing growth is global, extending from the U.S. to Europe to China.

In a gloomy editorial published, entitled *"Dealing with the evils of stagflation,"* the *Financial Times for June 2011* wrote: "Although the recovery has been much shallower than in past recessions, it is tailing off." The response of the international capitalist elite to the dire situation of most was to utilize the crisis to launch a counterrevolutionary offensive against the working class. "There are countless indices of growing social distress in the U.S. record levels of long-term unemployment, millions of home foreclosures, a 70 percent increase in Food Stamp rolls over the past three years, a jump of more than 20 percent in the number of people enrolled in Medicaid, the government health care program for the poor. But the response of the U.S. political elite - from the Obama administration to state and local governments - was to slash Medicaid, Food Stamps, Medicare and every other social program for workers, poor people and the elderly."(See: U.S. Job reports June 2011). At this same time, corporate America, was presently sitting on a cash hoard of $2 trillion, acquired through record profits and soaring stock prices achieved by means of wage cutting and virtually free credit from the Federal Reserve Board. CEO pay was again exploding, with corporate executives taking home millions a year and some hedge fund managers receiving billions.

HEALTH CARE – A *Look at conditions in 2011*

The Obama administration and congressional Republicans were conspiring to cut trillions of dollars in Medicare and Medicaid, the programs for the elderly and poor. One study estimates that a proposal from Republicans to cut Medicaid—which the Obama administration has refrained from publicly criticizing—would raise the number of people without coverage by 44 million over the next decade.

In 2011, under the Obama administration, this scorched earth policy entered a new phase. The first step was taken in 2010 under the guise of "health care reform," a drive to reduce corporate and government spending under the fraudulent slogan of "universal coverage." There was little attempt to hide the fact that what the administration was seeking was a sharp reduction in access to health care and other social programs. Obama's health care plan was filled with concessions for insurance companies. The president and his party had caved in to the drug companies on reimporting Canadian drugs, on negotiating drug prices downward and on generics. This explains why Big Pharma, the same people who ran the devastating series of anti-reform "Harry and Louise" ads to spike the Clinton-era drive to fix health care spent $100 million to run Obama ads using the president's language about "bipartisan" solutions to health care reform. The president and his party had received more money from private insurers and the for-profit health care industry than even Republicans, with the president alone taking $19 million in the 2008 election cycle alone, more than all his Republican, Democratic and independent rivals combined.

THE MESS OF DOMESTIC WELFARE- *A Look at conditions in 2009*

Of the 1%, by the 1%, for the 1%

Since the Obama administration there were over 4 million more Americans living in poverty and poor people make up 15.7 percent of the population, according to new figures for 2009 released by the U.S. Census Bureau on Wednesday. Taking into account living costs such as medical expenses, transportation and child care as well as non-cash benefits including Medicare, food stamps and low-income tax subsidies, the Census Bureau estimated there were 47.8 million people living in poverty in the U.S. in 2009

Among the sadistic statistic of that year was an increase of poverty for the elderly. According to the official poverty figures, 8.9 percent of those 65 and older were living in poverty in 2009. But when out-of-pocket medical costs and other expenses are taken into account, the elderly poverty rate nearly doubles to 16.1 percent. The highest poverty rate being among children, 18 percent of whom are poor, according to vastly underestimate the real level of poverty in the U.S., since they both use an income threshold that is absurdly low. The official 2009 poverty threshold was an annual income of $14,570 for family of two and $22,050 for a family of four. This reflects the indifference of the political and media establishment to the acute and worsening social distress in the country and the vast chasm separating the ruling elite from the mass of the people.

The Obama administration is spearheaded the attack on the domestic welfare, including extension of the Bush-era tax cuts for the rich, which will funnel some $70 billion a year into the coffers of the wealthiest 2 percent of the population, and the lowering of the estate tax, which will award some 6,600 families an estimated $23 billion in tax breaks. The Obama administration intensified the pro-corporate policies that have led to a massive growth of social inequality over the past three decades.   The Economic Policy Institute (EPI) reported that the wealth of the richest 1 percent of U.S. households in 2009 was 225 times greater than the median family net worth in America. The record figure underscores how the ruling elite have used the financial crisis and recession of 2011 to further plunder the social wealth. The ratio of the wealthiest 1 percent to median wealth last in 2010 was nearly twice the ratio of 125 in 1960 using new formula, Census Bureau ups estimate of US poverty rate to 15.7 percent; yet, as Columbia University professor Joseph E. Stiglitz comments in Vanity Fair, 1 percent of the people take nearly a quarter of the nation's income—an inequality even the wealthy will come to regret." **THE FAT AND THE FURIOUS**, the top 1 percent may have the best houses, educations, and lifestyles, says the author, but *"**their fate is bound up with how the other 99 percent live**.*"{*See: Of the 1%, by the 1%, for the 1% in vanityfair.*}

As the common worker and the poor cascade down the ugly but true side of the American nightmare, corporate profitability had rebounded, reaching the highest level ever, $1.68 trillion, in 2010, up 36.8 percent in a single year. Profits increased 61.5 percent from the low point in the 2008 financial crisis that triggered the ongoing economic slump. With the help of the Obama administration stocks and profits for the super-rich rebounded, with prices up 70 percent from the low point in 2008-2009, and a whopping $1 trillion added to stock values in 2010 alone. CEO pay went back to the stratospheric levels that prevailed before the crash, up 50 percent from 2009 to 2010, while pay levels for average workers have stagnated. All of the administration's policies represent a continuation and deepening of the rightwing policies of the Bush administration. The Obama administration expanded the bailout of Wall Street begun under the Bush administration, devoting the full resources of the federal treasury to rescuing the banks and safeguarding the accumulated wealth of the financial elite. Despite the announcing of a recovery and stimulus package for the mass of people, for the common person there was no recovery. Instead, the Obama administration spearheaded a drive by corporate America to make the mass pay for the financial crisis and bailout, through the destruction of seven million jobs, the slashing of pay and benefits, and an unprecedented attack on public services and social programs.

PUBLIC EDUCATION OR THE LACK OF IT

The American capitalist ruling class, by way of the deceptive mouthing of the Obama administration, proclaims that a major concern for the uplift of society and - according to Obama - the alternative to "reparations" for the African in America is by way of improving public education. Nevertheless, efforts by positive and progressive forces to improve public education in the U.S. for over 150 years, is being dismantled. Cities throughout the country are closing public schools, expanding private charter schools, increasing class sizes, laying off thousands of teachers, and imposing sharp cuts in pay and benefits. In response to cuts in state funding, public colleges and universities are raising tuition to levels unaffordable to the vast majority of working class youth. State governments have passed legislation targeting the basic right to collectively resist the demands of the corporations and states. Several states, including most recently the Democratic-controlled government in Massachusetts, have followed the lead of Wisconsin in passing laws that rip up existing contracts with state employees and prohibit strikes. This attack on public education had taken place at the same time as the sums of money controlled by the wealthy reach record highs. Corporate profits in the first quarter of that year broke the record set the previous quarter of $1.68 trillion at an annualized rate. CEO pay for 2010 exceeded the previous record levels set prior to the crash. The combined net wealth of just the 400 richest Americans was, over $1.37 trillion—approximately the same amount that would be saved over an entire decade through cuts in Medicaid that will threaten the lives and health of millions of people.

Obama has already been dubbed the "billion-dollar candidate," since his campaign was expected to be the first in U.S. history to raise and spend that enormous sum. The number is appropriate and symbolic, given that the Obama presidency has served the billionaires at the expense of millions. High rollers would be called upon to do even more in the 2012 campaign. This effort alone would give Obama a war chest of more than $150 million.

OBAMA and AFRICANS IN THE US- A *Look at conditions in 2011*

{African American unemployment remains at over 15 percent}

The two interesting facts below bring to light the loathe that Barak Obama has for his own people.

> 1. For African-American {Africans in America} unemployment remains at over 15%. as high as 66% for African {Black} youth

> 2. President Obama waded into the national race debate in an unlikely setting and with an unusual choice of words: telling daytime talk show hosts that African-Americans *are "sort of a mongrel people."* The president appeared on ABC's morning talk show "The View" Thursday, where he talked about the forced resignation of Agriculture Department official Shirley Sherrod, his experience with race and his roots.

Even system supporting conservatives such as Democratic Dr. Cornel West sees Obama as **a tool of the ruling class.** In an interview by RawReplay, Dr. West *suggested that Obama has sold out and become* **"a puppet"** *of powerful interests, merely promising change and not delivering*. Appearing on an MSNBC panel West remained outspoken. Amid a very heated discussion of whether President Obama is doing enough for Black people in America, he called the president ***"another black mascot" of "Wall Street oligarchs."***

THE INVASION OF LIBYA: THE REAL REASON[1]

---

[1] For more on this issue, updates and the Benghazi cover up ; See*: Chickens Come Home to Roost: A Critical Analysis of American Capitalism in Crisis*, by Gideon Odinga, 2014

On February 23, 2011 in a speech delivered with Secretary of State Clinton at his side, Obama announced that the government of the United States will soon intervene in Libya with its globalist partners under the threadbare cover of humanitarian aid and respect for human rights. True to his role as the first Black president of the U.S., Obama played his part as the mouth piece and voice of U.S. imperialism and hegemony, particularly as it relates to the new scramble for the riches , strategic location and resources of the most precious and expensive piece or real estate in the world, the continent of Africa. The U.S. has always hid its true intent of aggression behind a concealment of "**democracy**" – **demon nacracy**" and humanitarian concern. There is a historical precedent for such deceitfulness:

<u>The Sinking of the battleship Maine, 1898 – leading to the Spanish-American war.</u> Controversy still surrounds the sinking of the Maine. During this period America was about the business of building its' imperial power. It sought the control of the Western hemisphere. Of course such control trampled over the rights of the indigenous people, but America's aim was never justice but power. It was during this time that the iniquitous Monroe Doctrine was issued by President James Monroe. In essence, it stated that no European power could have dominance in the Western Hemisphere. In other words America was telling the world that we are the thieves of this area and no other thieves were welcomed. The problem was that there was another thief, called Spain, which still had imperial interest in Cuba. America sought an excuse to fight Spain and chose to create the image that it was aiding the legitimate struggle of freedom fighters in Cuba who were fighting a war of national liberation against Spanish imperialism. The basis of this liberation movement was African and Latino. The battleship main was sent into the harbor of Havana where it was mysteriously exploded. Spain denied it did it. In Edward P. McMorrow work, "What Destroyed the USS Maine-An Opinion", evidence is given implicating the hidden hand of America. America charged into war with Spain under the slogan, "Remember the Maine" " Senator Thurston of

Nebraska said "war with Spain would increase the business and earnings of every American railroad, it would increase the output of every American factory, and it would stimulate every branch of industry and domestic commerce." Major-General of volunteers, in order to annex the pearl of the Antilles". In this contrived war over 600, 000 died.,

The sinking of the Lusitania May 7, 1915 was a British-American plan to be co-conspirators in the deaths of its own citizens in order to create hysteria that would enable them to create a justification for America to enter the war. Although before 1915 America was trading with the "hated Nazi", after 1915, America saw it in their interest to come clearly on the side of Britain and France. After the war America would try to turn both France and England into American neo-colonies.

The Lusitania was a passenger ship. Years later it would be found that the Lusitania was carrying a large cache of arms that would be eventually used against Germany. By concealing them on the Lusitania, the allied forces could evade the very effective German blockade and submarine campaign. What is even more alarming is the fact that Churchill and Woodrow Wilson knew that it would be a very high probability that the ship would be in eminent danger, a fact that was concealed from the hundreds of passengers, many of whom were Americans. Ample evidence of this is given in Christopher's Hitchens book, " Blood, Class, and Nostalgia. He shows that Churchill plays a strong part in the sinking of the ship and the controversy of blaming the Germans. Of course America and England worked very close before and during the war. Both countries, by their silence and cunning, allowed the Lusitania to be in waters that would force Germany to sink the ship; however, Hitchens gives credible evidence that England - with American knowledge - sank the boat itself. This was used as one of the justification for America entering the war shortly after.

The Gulf of Tonkin Lie That Launched the Vietnam War 1964 "The official story was that North Vietnamese torpedo boats(PT) launched an "unprovoked attack" against a U.S. destroyer on "routine patrol" in the Tonkin Gulf on Aug. 2 and that North Vietnamese PT boats followed up with a "deliberate attack" on a pair of U.S. ships two days later. The truth was very different. Rather than being on a routine patrol Aug. 2, the U.S. destroyer Maddox was actually engaged in aggressive intelligence gathering maneuvers in sync with coordinated attacks on North Vietnam by the South Vietnamese navy and the Laotian air force. "The day before, two attacks on North Vietnam had taken place," writes scholar Daniel C. Hallin. Those assaults were "part of a campaign of increasing military pressure on the North that the United States had been pursuing since early 1964." On the night of Aug. 4, the Pentagon proclaimed that a second attack by North Vietnamese PT boats had occurred earlier that day in the Tonkin Gulf -- a reporter cited by President Johnson as he went on national TV that evening to announce a momentous escalation in the war: air strikes against North Vietnam.

But Johnson ordered U.S. bombers to "retaliate" for a North Vietnamese torpedo attack that never happened! Prior to the U.S. air strikes, top officials in Washington had reason to doubt that any Aug. 4 attack by North Vietnam had occurred. Cables from the U.S. task force commander in the Tonkin Gulf, Captain John J. Herrick, referred to "freak weather effects," "almost total darkness" and an "overeager sonar man" who "was hearing his ship's own propeller beat." One of the Navy pilots flying overhead that night was squadron commander James Stockdale, who gained fame later as a POW and then Ross Perot's vice presidential candidate. "I had the best seat in the house to watch that event," recalled Stockdale a few years ago, "and our destroyers were just shooting at phantom targets -- there were no PT boats there.... There was nothing there but black water and American firepower.

In 1965, Lyndon Johnson commented: "For all I know, our Navy was shooting at whales out there." But Johnson's deceitful speech of Aug. 4, 1964, won accolades from editorial writers. The president proclaimed the New York Times "went to the American people last night with the somber facts." The Los Angeles Times urged Americans to "face the fact that the Communists, by their attack on American vessels in international waters, have themselves escalated the hostilities." An exhaustive new book, The War Within: America's Battle over Vietnam begins with a dramatic account of the Tonkin Gulf incidents. In an interview, author Tom Wells told us that American media "described the air strikes that Johnson launched in response as merely `tit for tat' -- when in reality they reflected plans the administration had already drawn up for gradually increasing its overt military pressure against the North." Why such inaccurate news coverage? Wells points to the media's "almost exclusive reliance on U.S. government officials as sources of information" -- as well as "reluctance to question official pronouncements on 'national security issues.'" Daniel Hallin's classic book The "Uncensored War" observes that journalists had "a great deal of information available which contradicted the official account [of Tonkin Gulf events]; it simply wasn't used. The day before the first incident, Hanoi had protested the attacks on its territory by Laotian aircraft and South Vietnamese gunboats". Once again America had use lies to pave its way into war. One is not surprised that there are no weapons of mass destruction to be found in Iraq, although this was one of the main justification for America going to war, a war that will end in a victorious guerrilla struggle by the masses of Iraq. **THE FACTS SPEAK FOR THEMSELVES!**

Far from any humanitarian concerns or to the so-called justifiable rebels, the U.S. –NATO invasion and bombing of Libya **has all to do with Gold, oil, preventing an United Africa with a single currency based on gold, The fall of the U.S. dollar, U.S. fight for survival, The new scramble for Africa, and the Obama strategy and Africa.**

First of all only the most naive and poorest student of history would not know that NATO from its inception in 1949 was founded to counter the Soviet Union and its satellite states in Eastern Europe. The U.S.-NATO coordinated relentless bombardment of Tripoli represents a new stage in one of the most naked acts of imperialist aggression since the wars of conquest launched by Hitler and Mussolini in the 1930s. Hundreds of people have been killed and thousands wounded. The bombings have demolished civilian government buildings, while damaging homes, hospitals and schools. Their intended collateral effect is to terrorize Tripoli's population of 1.7 million.

In an earlier period, such air attacks were described as "terror bombings." They were carried out by Hitler's Luftwaffe against defenseless populations—in Guernica during the Spanish Civil War in 1937, in Warsaw in 1939, in Rotterdam in 1940 and in Belgrade in 1941—with the aim of annihilating the targeted country's armed forces, destroying its state and breaking the morale of all those opposed to foreign occupation. Acting under the pretense of enforcing a UN resolution and protecting civilian life, the US and its allies have caused immense suffering among Libyan civilians. They have likewise jettisoned the essential contents of the UN's founding charter, which outlawed wars of aggression and upheld the principle of national sovereignty, barring intervention in the domestic affairs of member states. Those responsible for these acts--Barrack Obama, David Cameron, Nicolas Sarkozy and others--are guilty of war crimes.

The Jamahiriya {People's Republic} of Libya in its current national and Pan-African perspective represents a serious threat to the Western imperialist and Zionist powers. The statement of Minister Louis Farrakhan in the " last Updated: June 7, 2011, Final call newspaper is quite informative as to the real motive of the U.S. and NATO "If they kill Brother Gadhafi, I submit to you that American interests in Africa will come under severe strain,"…" "That man has invested in Africa more than any other leader in the recent history of Africa's coming into political independence," he continued. The Muslim leader said America needs access to the mineral resources in Africa to be a viable power in the 21st century. "How's America's wealth today? How is she doing financially? What is the deficit? Some say it's about $56 trillion counting Social Security and Medicare. That's a big number. She's printing money, but there's nothing backing it," said Min. Farrakhan.

In the book, "The Fall of America," the Most Honorable Elijah Muhammad wrote, "One of the greatest powers of America was her dollar. The loss of such power will bring any nation to weakness, for this is the media of exchange between nations." ""Gadhafi's creation of the African Investment Bank in Sirte (Libya) and the African Monetary Fund to be based in Cameroon will supplant the IMF and undermine Western economic hegemony in Africa," said Gerald Pereira, an executive board member of the former Tripoli-based World Mathaba.

Such a move by Tripoli would also spell bad news for France because when the African Monetary Fund and the African Central Bank in Nigeria starts printing gold-backed currency, it would "ring the death knell" for the CFA franc through which Paris was able to maintain its neocolonial grip on 14 former African colonies for the last 50 years.

"The AU {African Union} was the framework the Libyan leader was using to establish African self-determination and economic self-sufficiency. Col. Gadhafi financed the restructuring of the former Organization of African Unity—formed by African leaders Dr. Kwame Nkrumah of Ghana, Sekou Toure of Guinea, Gamal Abdel Nasser of Egypt and others—into the AU and revived the concept of a United States of Africa with one continental army and a single currency backed by gold."

Obama put forward a narrative of the events leading up to the Libyan intervention that was false from start to finish.

"For more than four decades," he said, "the Libyan people have been ruled by a tyrant—Muammar Gaddafi." Last month, he continued, "Libyans took to the streets to claim their basic rights," but Gaddafi began "attacking his own people." While Obama decreed that Gaddafi had lost "the legitimacy to lead," the Libyan leader refused to listen, prompting Washington to go the UN Security Council to obtain a resolution authorizing "all necessary measures to protect the Libyan people."

Obama claimed that the U.S. military action had been carried out "to stop the killing" and had successfully "stopped Gaddafi's deadly advance." In reality, Washington has intervened in a civil war that it played no small role in fomenting. The U.S. Air Force along with smaller numbers of warplanes provided by Washington's NATO allies has functioned as the air force of the rebels, obliterating from the air troops loyal to the government in Tripoli, thereby clearing the way for the U.S.-backed forces on the ground.

This is another deception. Placing military operations in Libya under formal NATO command no more removes the U.S. from playing the decisive role than the formal command of NATO in Afghanistan makes the war there any less of a U.S. operation. NATO is dominated by the U.S. military, which will continue to play the decisive role in the attack on Libya. Even as the Obama administration was talking about the winding down of U.S. military operations, the Washington Post reported Monday that the Pentagon has deployed AC-130 and A-10 attack planes. These are aerial gunships that are used to massacre ground troops with heavy machine guns and cannons. As the Post noted, the deployment was an indication that the U.S. military has "been drawn deeper into the chaotic fight in Libya."

Moreover, the U.S. ruling elite viewed with increasing alarm the signs that both Russia and China were establishing connections with Libya, in terms of oil deals, infrastructure projects and arms contracts, which threatened U.S. interests in the Mediterranean and North Africa. The aim of the military action was to install a more pliant regime—an out-and-out U.S. puppet—in Tripoli. In the book I go into much more detail of the U.S. Strategy for Africa and the role a " Black " president plays I this nefarious stratagem

Under the name of many U.S. presidential administrations, humanity has suffered. The U.S. presidency and those who seek the oval office are only the face that people see. *Obama is not the power but only the face that the power seeks to hide behind and so - as I have said before - **this analysis is far beyond Obama**.* It is an analysis that goes to the heart of the beast. It has been said that the greatest of the sins is not to show appreciation. The U.S. capitalist system has committed many sins against humanity, and it has so very often hid its deeds of devastating devilish intent behind a smiling face. **But smiling faces can tell lies!**

Part two

We will focus on the domestic strategy of America's neo-liberal ruling class; a ruling class that is frantically trying to devise and implement the maintenance and expansion of a foreign and domestic strategy that it has been hell bent on since 1945. This strategy has went under many names: "save the world from communism", *"the Truman Doctrine"*, *"Stop the Domino Theory in Viet Nam and South East Asia"*, *"The New World Order"*, *"Desert Storm"*, *"the War on Terror"*, *"Globalization"* and we can be assured that the next administration - **and the current ruling class that supports and backs the next administration** - will also develop some "high sounding rhetoric" to hide its sewer low initiative of trying to oppress the peoples of the world. Whatever the name, the strategy must include a domestic and international line of attack.

The Obama campaign, in terms of its projected "media image" and aims, as well as the intent of the hand of deception that controls the puppet strings , has a definite intent regarding the domestic situation inside of the U.S., a situation that could turn ugly and radical given the inevitable contradictions that are developing domestically and internationally. The domestic strategy is a vital complement to both the international strategy and foreign policy of U.S. imperialism; in both cases, it is a strategy based on a situation of desperation!

Externally and internally, the U.S. ruling class must give the impression of change and reform while attempting to come to grips with the inevitable contradictions of a contracting empire and an empire that finds itself in the whirlwinds of competition and contestation from rivalry capitalist powers in western and eastern Europe as well as antagonism from the capitalist intentions of an awakening giant in Asia

(China) - a giant that has a vested interest in building more and more with the tyrannical eastern "capitalist" bear Russia. ***One cannot adequately analyze or understand the Obama drama without having a correct analysis and understanding of U.S. capitalism and imperialism.***

"Modern capitalism has grown out of a horrid history and legacy of cultural disrespect, greed, racism, oppression, exploitation, conquest, invasion and a barbarism unmatched in the sordid history of tyranny and anti-people State sponsor terror. While modern capitalism has used its accelerated technology to amazing heights, it has – on the negative side - corrupted itself and morally degraded itself to the slime of the most depraved toxic swamp. The dialectic of U.S. development is very unique. America is the most technologically advance society in the world today and at the same time the most politically backward society in the world today. America's insanity clearly is in the fact that it feeds on itself and will sell to itself the noose that will be used to hang itself. Historically oppressive empires try to give the impression that they are invulnerable and that their power is uncontestable. Yet, history shows clearly that empires come and go, rise and fall and are eventually brought down by their own evil endeavors, along with the triumphant struggles of those whom they have oppressed. Martin L. King would never tire of saying, ***"The moral arm of the universe is long but it bends towards justice."*** History also shows that when oppressive empires fall, they disintegrate astonishingly quick! The American capitalist empire – and the myth of anointed Obama - will be no exception to this historical maxim. Not even technologically advanced and "sophisticate" America and not even media made Obama will be able to avoid the destiny with history. The conscious mind and trained eye, already has seen the genesis-doom and major tumbling of the pillars of American capitalism and imperialism. The political-economic crisis, which currently is strangling all capitalist nations, and the present crisis in the international situation foretells the requiem that will surely befall the American government and its economy of doom no matter who the smiling face in the oval office is. **The "justice" forces of history will reclaim history, soon and very soon!"** [2]

The current international financial and political situation of world capitalism is characterized by a large quantity of destabilization, political-economic uncertainty, military expansion and at the same time military defeat and setbacks, a rising world condemnation and isolation, a growing anti-war movement within America and around the world, a decomposition of the anti-terror coalition organized by America, ground swelling distrust of the American ruling class, devastating setbacks in Afghanistan and Iraq, a mass "socialist-directed" upsurge in Latin America, intensified class and anti-neo-colonial struggle in Africa, a razor-sharp growth of mass revolutionary movements in Africa and throughout the Caribbean and Latin America, the growth of an American police state, an over stretched suicide prone U.S. military, a critical rising unemployment - that is a crisis in the communities of color within America, a deteriorating heath situation among the American citizenry – particularly in the communities of color, a dilapidated housing market, a government bail out of the housing mortgage industry that favors the super-rich and condemns the middle and lower classes, an international banking and finance crisis, the beginnings of an anti-racist-anti-capitalist African and Latino youth movement in the U.S., an American military intervention which attacks popular governments around the world, neo-liberal and neo-fascist policies and an intensification of race-class struggle in the color communities of the world.

Things are not going well for American capitalism or any of the G-8 capitalist countries, in fact nothing has gone right or well for them for some time, and the current situation only increases the problems geometrically for the enemy of the peoples of the world. ***"CHICKENS WILL COME HOME TO "ROOST"*** The Obama drama is an attempt at distraction and tentative reform. It is an illusion and distraction as

---

[2] ; See: Chickens Come Home to Roost: A Critical Analysis of American Capitalism in Crisis, by Gideon Odinga, 2013, Amazon

much as a super bowl, NBA series, movies, and crack cocaine; the illusion will only last for a very brief period and then reality, depression, frustration and rage will surely follow. .

At the very moment that American capitalism appears to be resilient, at the very moment that the oppressors gives the false impression of permanency and being at their zenith, at the height of the Obama drama, at the time that international finance capitalism manipulates its media and bourgeois scholars to portray a rose-colored picture of stability and growth, <u>imperialism is entering its decisive period of decline, and empires fall quickly!</u>

"For the day of the LORD is near upon the heathen: as thou hast done, it shall be done unto thee." Obadiah 1: 15

As bourgeoisie economist and campaign tricksters matched media hype with grand illusions of "things are really getting better<u>", a new face was being applied to the Frankenstein monster of American capitalism in the form of "Obama" But</u> the beast will not be hid for long. What better way to *con-psych* the people than a Black president? It is the old capitalist bait and switch game and unfortunately many are swallowing the con, hook, line, sinker and Obama drama. But who is this new bait and what hole did this worm crawl out of? Moreover, how did they make this particular maggot so, butterfly attractive? **"It's all in the packaging folk!"**

The making and marketing of Barack Obama:

Image and identity in U.S. politics

With the exception of a popular sham showing in Chicago, the thinking and personality of Sen. Barack Obama, the presumptive Democratic Party candidate for president, was known by only an elite few just a few years ago. For Africans in America *{Black U.S. citizens}*, most did not know Barak Obama from a can of paint!

Our brother Barak was born August 4, 1961 at the beginning of the turbulent and system shaking 1960's. Barak benefited from the mass struggle of the sixties which stood on the stalwart shoulders of the legacy of Black culture and resistance. His matriculation into Columbia University and Harvard Law School *(where he kept far away from mass struggle, mass issues and mass activism and interests)* was due not only to grade point average but mass resistance and mass bloodshed. As the *"Times"* noted, Obama, "whether out of professorial reserve or budding political caution," refused to take a stand on controversial issues. Also "he was unwilling to put his name to anything that could haunt him politically... – like strong support or involvement in Black issues! 'He figured out, you lay low; moreover, while in school and continuing in his political career he kept distance from mass issues or direct theoretical or activist confrontation with racism and economic exploitation issues. It's no surprise that he had little or nothing to say concerning Black people and the massacre of New Orleans, Jena Six, or Shean the Bell horror. But those who struggle for freedom must be willing to stand up for their rights! Laying low in racist Amerikkka will only get you buried further in disgrace and marginalized into shadows of obscurity;! Had it not been for the blood and struggle of the masses of African people, Barak would not have gotten near Ivy League academic status? Many in the African bourgeoisie elite own their success to Black mass nationalistic resistance!

After a primary victory in March 2004, Obama delivered the keynote address at the Democratic National Convention in July 2004. He was elected to the Senate in November 2004 with 70% of the vote. As a member of the Democratic minority in the 109th Congress, he helped create legislation to control conventional weapons and to promote greater public accountability in the use of federal funds. He also made official trips to Eastern Europe, the Middle East, and Africa. During the 110th Congress, he helped create legislation regarding lobbying and electoral fraud, climate change, nuclear terrorism, and care for returned U.S. military personnel. After announcing his presidential campaign in February 2007, Obama emphasized withdrawing American troops from

Iraq, energy independence, decreasing the influence of lobbyist, and promoting universal health care as top national priorities. ***In Obama's legislative history there is no outstanding emphasis or advocacy for civil rights, human rights or mass Black concerns.***

Yes! He is to be applauded for his academic proficiency and marginal community activism, but his appreciation for the mass struggle - that forced open the Ivy League doors and system political legislative prospects - falls disgustingly far away from the contributions of such African legislatures as the Black reconstruction legislators or the moderate and radical legislators of the 1960's period that provide Obama with the opportunities that allowed him to be in position to announce his candidacy for the oval office of U.S. imperialism. **The worse sin one can make is not to show appreciation!** As David Walsh describes " Obama is the product of identity politics, which came to prominence in the 1970s. This opportunist trend, promoted by sections of the ruling elite, elevated race or gender above class position and served to undermine any organized struggle of working and poor people against their social oppression. It became a way for a relatively a small section of blacks, Latinos and women to advance themselves at the expense of the mass. Obama's right wing ideological persuasion and right wing enthusiasm is seen in the light of these statements:

Obama was largely shaped by the sharp rightward shift in American ruling class policy that began in the late 1970s under Jimmy Carter and fully flowered during the Reagan administration. He was an impressionable 19 year old, a college student in Los Angeles, at the time of Reagan's first election. In *The Audacity of Hope,* Obama offers this remarkable tribute: "All of which may explain why, as disturbed as I might have been by Ronald Reagan's election in 1980... I understood his appeal... Reagan spoke to America's longing for order, our need to believe that we are not simply subject to blind, impersonal forces but that we can shape our individual and collective destinies, so long as we rediscover the traditional virtues of hard work, patriotism, personal responsibility, optimism, and faith.

Obama Says He Opposes "Slavery Reparations, Apology"

Fewer things in this world are more justifiable than the moral basis and humanistic sentiment and aspiration of reparations for the victims of the Atlantic - racist-capitalism – Slave trade, a crime against humanity. Even capitalist give forked tongue lip service to the demand for reparations; notwithstanding the fact that what one loses on the battle field can only be regained on the battlefield. The world-wide reparation movement by Africans is supported heavily by the masses of the people just as the demands of the civil-rights movement were supported by the masses of the people; yet the "anointed one" is vehemently opposed to reparations. ***Tom-cat, ain't going to do nothing that masa don't like!*** On this issue the "anointed one" comes up like a sacrilegious garbage can maggot! **Obama is a strategy of deception!** *{See: Obama Says He Opposes Slavery Reparations, Apology by Christopher Wills ;Associated Press August 2, 2008}*

Obama says that 'government should instead combat the legacy of slavery by improving schools, health care and the economy for all. I have said in the past — and I'll repeat again — that the best reparations we can provide are good schools in the inner city and jobs for people who are unemployed," But this is not a position Obama adopted just for the presidential campaign. He voiced the same concerns about reparations during his successful run for the Senate in 2004. *{See: Obama Opposes Slavery Reparations; USAtoday.com}*

Some two dozen members of Congress are co-sponsors of legislation to create a commission that would study reparations — that is, payments and programs to make up for the damage done by slavery. The National Association for the Advancement of Colored People supports the legislation, too. Cities around the country, including Obama's home of Chicago, have endorsed the idea, and so has a major union, the American Federation of State, County and Municipal Employees. Obama has an embarrassing and consistent record of not acting, advocating or moving in the interest of the masses of Black people. Of course this is a requirement to be a **Tom-cat!**

Obama – Tom cat and Tom Pawn
in implementation of strategy to
negate Black nationalism and ethnic cleansing

Relative to this discussion of a U.S. domestic strategy and Obama Drama is the content and genocidal implications of an article by Glen Ford in response to an article in the New York Times, entitled, " Is Obama the End of Black Politics? When considering Ford's comment the malicious strategy of U.S. domestic colonialism is very apparent

" The Sunday magazine of the nation's most influential newspaper predicts that Black politics as we know it is headed for extinction, that Barack Obama's **"brand of 'race-neutrality'** shows Black politics is obsolete, and should be abandoned." Of course, that's wishful thinking from a hostile quarter, based on assumptions that all Black politics is electoral, Blacks are becoming more conservative, and a generational crisis deeply divides Black America - none of which is true. However, Blacks have been set up for a fall." To the extent that African Americans expect more from Barack Obama than they got from Bill Clinton, they will be devastatingly disappointed."*{See: {New York Times Attempts to Define and Dictate Black Politics: by BAR executive editor Glen Ford}*

Barack Obama has a multiplicity of allegiances, and the specific needs of Black People are not near the top of his list. Again Mr. Ford comments:

"I would like to suggest that this country is already fascist and will only get more so in the future...for example look at the statistics about the incarceration of Africans...1 in 9 of every brother from 30-39 is in a U.S. jail or prison, and 1 out of every 100 people in this country are imprisoned not to speak of the extra judicial killings, lynching's, general racial profiling, the increase militarization and military aggression, for example the sending of U.S. war ships off of Lebanon to harass the Hezbollah and Syrian elements, lastly as Malcolm taught us so well, unity among our people does not mean acceptance of fifth column elements. Conscious Africans have to have the courage to expose and oppose all those who are in the pockets or our enemies...Malcolm in fact told a story about how a young Chinese woman shot her father for being a traitor to the revolution there and said that this is the way to deal with Toms...now we must all decide are we with Malcolm, are we with Kwame Ture, are we with Lumumba, Seku Ture, Robert Sobukwe, Nkrumah or are we with the handpicked lackeys of white supremacy such as Obama, who is the creation of the Chicago Democratic Machine (the new version headed up by the son ... that is why Bill Daley, the brother of the current mayor is an important member of his campaign.). Our people should ask themselves, why Obama has never done anything about the police killings of our people in Chicago, why he has never said anything about the seizure of the property and destruction of the African communities in Chicago, and as I have been a resident of Chicago all of my life, indeed I lived and maintain a business office in the Hyde Park area that he represented in the State Senate, I know firsthand his treachery... I will say this ... and this is the only thing I have positive to say about him, he did oppose the beginning of the war while he was in the state senate; however that is more of a reflection of the general position in Illinois and particularly Chicago, as for example the Chicago City Council voted to end the war...any way below you will find some info on McKinney's efforts with the Power to the People presidential campaign. An Obama presidency (or a Clinton presidency, should her campaign ultimately prevail), would thus represent a fine-tuning or adjustment in American foreign policy, but no let-up in American imperialism's drive to war and conquest, which arises not out of the brains of George W. Bush and Richard Cheney, but out of the historical crisis of American and world capitalism. Obama is merely the product of an effective marketing campaign which has utilized media outlets ranging from Rupert Murdoch to *The Nation* to sell this new version of a very old product—the Democratic Party "friend of the people," previously incarnated in the "insurgent" candidacy of Jimmy Carter in 1976, then in the "man from Hope," Bill Clinton himself, in 1992. An Obama presidency would no more represent a fundamental change in American politics than the election of Carter and Clinton did, and if Murdoch." *{New York Times Attempts to Define and Dictate Black Politics by BAR executive editor Glen Ford}*

Obama's Policy Solutions - or more accurately the policy solutions that the Obama campaign - has been given and advised to - mouthed by the U.S. ruling class are contradictory and forked tongued demagoguery. Obama policy solutions point in opposite directions. Consider some of his promises:

> rebuilding our roads and schools, taking care of our veterans and sending our children to college - **How can this be done without drastically slashing the war budget? It can't.** Obama is not thinking about cutting the war budget but increasing it and he is for expanding the war in Afghanistan, where – by the way – the U.S. is experiencing a drastic defeat, as is the **case in Iraq!**

> **How about providing jobs for all at a living wage? Can this be done without breaking with all the corporate "free trade" and privatization agreements? It can't.** Obama walked out of the room during the U.S.-Peru FTA vote in Congress last summer -- so as not to upset his labor constituents -- but he praised the bill in the media, just as hc praised "free trade" in his private meetings with Canadian political leaders prior to the Ohio primary. Obama, like Clinton, is a supporter of NAFTA, CAFTA and "free trade(free doom"

> How about providing healthcare for all? **Can this be done without removing the private insurance companies from the healthcare equation?**

> Obama says he is the man to stand up to injustice and he is the anointed one with courage to answer the red phone in some twilight hour but he allowed the racist U.S. ruling class to "punk him out" to the point that he denounced his own pastor for telling the simple TRUTH. Obama responds and jumps through hoops for the ones who really rule American capitalism.*{Who Rules America: by G. William*

Domhoff; Also see: The Rich and the Super-Rich: A Study in the Power of Money Today: by Ferdinand Lundberg}

Obama the running pathetic dog of Zionism

Dr. Kwame Ture, correctly states that, "The litmus test of genuine revolutionary activity is anti-Zionism." Anti-Zionist or even pro-Zionism can be a barometer to assess, evaluate and even predict political behavior and moral viability of activist, organizations, movements, elected officials, ministers/religious-spiritual leaders, presidents and presidential candidates - **the two latter being historically "park ape enthusiastic" in support of morally filthy Zionism**. Zionism, Zionist strategy and Israeli domestic and foreign policy decision and decisional results*{ operating within the policy of other governments and within the settler colony of Israel }* have not only been terroristically overwhelming, demoralizing and devastating to African people worldwide, but they have also been a scourge to humanity.*{See: Zionism in the Age of the Dictators, by Lenni Brenner}* There is overwhelming and crushing evidence to the Zionist's military, political and financial backing of the worst crime against humanity and African people, the Atlantic Slave Trade. According to Dr. Leonard Jeffries, 75% of the financing of the Atlantic Slave Trade was supplied by morally bankrupt Zionism.*{See; Our Sacred Mission: speech at the Empire State Black Arts and Cultural Festival in Albany, New York, July 20, 1991, by Dr. Leonard Jeffries. Also see: The Secret Relationship Between Blacks and Jews, Volume I, published by the Nation of Islam}* Any Black elected official that bows before zones (and **_the majority of them do_**) is puke treacherous and despicable to the depths of the lowest contempt! Obama goes beyond bowing; he prostrates himself before Zionism. When the Zionist tell him to jump his reply is how high boss and should I perform flips in the air and hit the ground running to lap up your vomit. The proof of such an acid criticism is an empirical fact! In a rough transcript that came from the Obama campaign of a closed meeting that the candidate held, in Cleveland, Obama proudly stated:

"*I will also carry with me an unshakable commitment to the security of Israel and the friendship between the United States and Israel.* The U.S. Israel relationship is rooted in shared interests, shared values,

shared history and in deep friendship among our people. It is supported by a strong bipartisan consensus that I am proud to be a part of and I will work tirelessly as president to uphold and enhance the friendship between the two countries. The people of Israel showed their courage and commitment to democracy every day that they board a bus or kiss their children goodbye or argue about politics in a local café. And I know how much Israelis crave peace. I know that Prime Minister Olmert was elected with a mandate to pursue it."{<u>The Power of Israel in the United States,</u> *by James Petras. Clarity Press, 2006}*

This is the same cat (Tom cat) that rejected, repudiated and denounced reparations for his own people. "Puke treacherous" are words much too kind to label Obama! Tom cat goes even further to say:

"I pledge to make every effort to help Israel achieve that peace. I will strengthen Israel's security and strengthen Palestinian partners who support that vision and personally work for two states that can live side by side in peace and security with Israel's status as a Jewish state ensured so that Israelis and Palestinians can pursue their dreams. I also expect to work on behalf of peace with the full knowledge that Israel still has bitter enemies who are intent on its destruction. We see their intentions every time a suicide bomber strikes, we saw their intentions with the katusha rockets that Hezbollah rained down on Israel from Lebanon in 2006 and we see it today in the Kasams that Hamas fires into Israel every single day from as close as Gaza or as far as Tehran. The Defense cooperation between the United States to Israel"

It is clear who's interest Obama is primarily concerned with. But let us consider more The American ruling class and Obama's primary concern and support of Israel by looking at Zionism's and Israel's power and influence within American capitalism and world imperialism.

The power and influence of Zionism and Israel inside the U.S. and within other world capitalist powers and puppet regimes is pretentious and formidable. Zionism is clearly a major form of imperialism, and has played a role in imperialism powers even before the infamous World Zionist congress meeting in Basil Switzerland in 1897 and it has played a major role ever since. . *{See: Zionism in the Age of the Dictators, by Lenni Brenner}*

Consider the facts from a research by James Petras, "*The Power of Israel in the United* States. **"Clarity Press, 2006,**

J.J. Goldberg in his book, *Jewish Power Inside the Jewish Establishment* based on data in the early, 1990's, noted that 45 percent of the fundraising for the Democratic Party and 25 percent of the funding for the Republicans came from Jewish-funded Political Action Committees (PACs). No single other lobby including Big Pharmacy, Big Oil and Agro-business plays such a dominant financial role in party funding.

p14

The basis of the [Jewish] Lobby's PAC power is rooted in the high proportion of Jewish families among the wealthiest families in the United States. According to Forbes, 25 to 30 percent of US multi-millionaires and billionaires are Jewish. If we add the contributions to the Lobby by Jewish-Canadian billionaires with assets worth over 30 percent of the Canadian Stock Market, we can realize the scope and depth of the Lobby's power to dictate Middle East policy to Congress and the Executive.

p15
Who Finances the State of Israel?

The question of who is financing the Israeli state is basic because Israel as we know it today is not a viable state without massive external support. As the July 2004 updated Congressional Research Service Issue Brief for Congress titled "Israel: U.S. Foreign Assistance" points out in its opening statement: "Israelis not economically self-sufficient, and relies on foreign assistance and borrowing to maintain its economy. 1126 Despite what might seem an insurmountable obstacle not just to Israel's prosperity, but to its sustainability, the country has nonetheless done rather well. Billions of dollars are raised from a variety of Jewish and non-Jewish institutions to sustain the Israeli war machine, its policy of generous subsidies for Jews enticed to settle in colonies in the Occupied Territories and in Israel-sufficient to place the country as the world's 28th highest in living standards for Israel's Jewish citizens.

Without external aid Israel's economy would require severe cutbacks in living standards and working conditions, leading to the likely flight of most Israeli professionals, businessmen, and recent overseas immigrants. The Israeli military budget would be reduced and Israel would be obligated to reduce its military interventions in the Arab East and the Occupied Territories. Israel would cease being a renter state living on overseas subsidies and would be obligated to engage in productive activity-a return to farming, manufacture and services minus the exploitation of low paid Asian maids, imported Eastern European farm workers, and Palestinian construction laborers.

In the United States there are essentially four basic sources of financial, ideological and political support for the Israeli renter economy:

1. Wealthy Jewish contributors and powerful disciplined fund-raising organizations.

2. The U.S. government-both Congress and the Presidency.

3. The mass media, particularly the New York Times, Hollywood, and the major television networks.

4. The trade union bosses and the heads of pension funds.

There is substantial overlap in these four institutional configurations. For example, Jewish supporters in the Israeli lobby work closely with Congressional leaders to secure long-term, large-scale US military and economic aid for Israel. Most of the mass media and a few trade unions are influenced by unconditional supporters of the Israeli war machine. Pro-Israel Jews are disproportionately represented in the financial, political, professional, academic, real estate, insurance and mass media sectors of the American economy. While Jews are a minority in each and every one of these categories, their disproportionate power and influence stems from the fact that they function collectively: they are organized, active, and concentrate on a single issue-US policy in the Middle East, and specifically in securing Washington's massive, unconditional, and continuing military, political and financial support for Israel. Operating from their strategic positions in the power structure, they are able to influence policy and censor any dissident commentators or views from circulating freely in the communications and political system.

> Support for Israel from the U.S. government

The data below, compiled by the CRS [Congressional Research Service] Issue Brief in 2004, provide some notion of the extent of U.S. aid and special features.

* Israel has received more than $90 billion in U.S. aid up to 2003, of which $75 billion has been in grants (i.e. nonrepayable), and $15 billion in loans.

* Since 1985, the United States has provided $3 billion in grants annually to Israel.

* Resettlement assistance for Soviet immigrants peaked in 1992 at $80 million, but continues to be subsidized at $60 million for 2003, $50 million in 2004 and again in 2005.

* In 1990, Israel requested $10 billion in loan guarantees, which would enable Israel to borrow from U.S. commercial establishments, with their loans guaranteed against default by the US government. In 2004, a further $9 billion in loan guarantees was included in FL. 1088-11.

ONE CANNOT BE PRO ISRAEL AND PRO BLACK AT THE SAME TIME. ONE CANNOT BE DOUBLE MINDED AND WAVERING ON THIS ISSUE. ONE CANNOT SERVE GOD AND THE DEVIL AT THE SAME TIME

INDICATORS OF HYPOCRITICAL INSENSITIVITY AND GROWING CALAMITY

The following are more examples of non-compassion of U.S. capitalism and reinforces the idea that *one cannot be a good president of an evil political-economy.* The dollar figures given show the abyss of disregard and the chasm of depravity of the U.S, government and the executive office that would tolerate such immorality

- ❖ The money spent on war each day is enough to enroll an additional 58,000 children in head start each year, or make a year's college affordable for 160,000 low income students through Pell grants {
  {See:http://www.nytimes.com/2008/03/04/opinion/04herbert.html}
- ❖ 13 Million U.S. Children go Hungry each day! The Cost of one B-1 bomber $200 million. One in six Americans is fighting hunger. In 2008, 17 million households, 14.6 percent of households (approximately one in seven), were food insecure, the highest number ever recorded in the United States. Four million households became food insecure in 2008, the largest increase ever recorded (p. iii, USDA 2008). (To get population figures from family size figures, multiply family size numbers by 2.58, the average family size.) In 2008, 39.8 million people were in poverty, up from 37.3 million in 2007 -- the second consecutive annual increase in the number of people in poverty *{Census Bureau 2010).{ Also see: Hunger in America: 2011 United states Hunger and poverty facts; World hunger service. }*

- For FY 2008, the Bush administration had requested $647.3 billion to cover the costs of national defense but just **$5.2 billion a year: is** the estimate for direct assistance to the most nutritionally deprived people on earth (Those starving to death- 214 million people. This has only grown worse with the Obama administration
- The U.S. unjust war in Iraq and Afghanistan has cost " currently" **$864 billion**
- The cost of two B-1 Bombers **(two hundred million)** could end child hunger in the U.S.! The cost of the Iraq and Afghanistan conflicts have grown to a staggering proportion of three trillion dollars

Poverty is the leading cause of hunger in America. Over 37 million people in the United States live below the poverty line and are at risk of hunger.

- 12.5 percent of the nation's population lived in poverty in 2007.

- In 2007, the poverty rate for families was 9.8 percent, comprising 7.6 million families.
- The poverty rate in 2007 for American children under 18 was 18.0 percent, up from 17.4 percent in 2006.

- 14 million children live in poverty in the U.S.
- The U.S. poverty rate for people 65 and over is 9.7 percent; 3.5 million elderly live in poverty.
- Of all family groups, poverty is highest among those headed by single women.

Study: Poverty dramatically affects children's brains
By Greg Toppo, USA TODAY

A new study finds that certain brain functions of some low-income 9- and 10-year-olds pale in comparison with those of wealthy children and that the difference is almost equivalent to the damage from a stroke. "It is a similar pattern to what's seen in patients with strokes that have led to lesions in their prefrontal cortex," which controls higher-order thinking and problem solving, says lead researcher Mark Kishiyama, a cognitive psychologist at the University of California-Berkeley . "It suggests that in these kids, prefrontal function is reduced or disrupted in some way."

- As a whole, U.S. cities report that they are not able to meet the need for providing shelter for homelessness persons have a limited ability to meet the need for emergency food assistance.
- An estimated 24 to 27 million people in the U.S. turned to hunger relief agencies in 2006.
- 35.9% of American households receiving food from food banks, shelters and pantries have one or more adults employed. The cost of direct U.S. military operations - not even including long-term costs such as taking care of wounded veterans - already exceeds the cost of the 12-year war in Vietnam and is more than double the cost of the Korean War. And, even in the best case scenario, these costs are projected to be almost ten times the cost of the first Gulf War, almost a third more than the cost of the Vietnam War, and twice that of the First World War. The only war in our history which cost more was the Second World War, when 16.3 million U.S. troops fought in a campaign lasting four years, at a total cost (in 2007 dollars, after adjusting for inflation) of about $5 trillion (that's $5 million, or £2.5 million). With virtually the entire armed forces committed to fighting the Germans and Japanese, the cost per troop (in today's dollars) was less than $100,000 in 2007 dollars. By contrast, the Iraq war is costing upward of $400,000 per troop.

Chapter Three   The U.S. Foreign Policy and Neo-Liberalism

"After reading the harrowing account of the brutalities of slavery, of subjugation, of deprivation and humiliation when whole civilizations were crushed in order to serve the imperialist interests of the West, when settled societies were disintegrated by force of imperialist arms so that the plantation owners of the "new World" could get their uprooted and therefore permanent labor force to build what was now the most advanced capitalist economy, it become absolutely clear that the only way out of our current impasse is through a revolutionary path- a complete break with the system which is responsible for all our past and present misery." A.M. BaBu from the Postscript of ***How Europe Underdeveloped Africa*** by Walter Rodney

"For evil doers shall be cut off:

But those who wait on the Lord; HE shall renew their strength.

They shall inherit the earth."

(From the book of Psalms 37 and Isaiah 40)

Oh! If only those who made wars had to fight them; **and Oh! If U.S. presidents and those who sought and seek that despotic office only had to pay for the wars they declared and the foreign policies they have endorsed and "mouthed to the people of America and the world,"** then perhaps historic justice would roll down like a mighty stream! But they will pay, as America must pay for the decades of deceit and the years of misery it has caused for millions!

In the name of the U.S. presidency and under the misleading banner of democracy (demon -nocracy) , battleships and bombs, armies and arsenals, greed and malicious intentions have invaded the sanctities of cultures, and devastated the sovereignties of governments, all in the name of U.S. imperialism! This fact alone would make any sane, honest and morally responsible person look on the office of the American presidency with derision, disgust and disassociation. Dr. Martin Luther

King describe it with glowing moral insight when he said, "My own country is the greatest purveyor of violence in the world. *(See: "Why I oppose the war in Viet Nam:" by Dr. M.L. King Jr.)*

With totalitarian and racist disrespect and "a-moral' sadistic savagery , the history of U.S. foreign policy and U.S. relations with Africans and Africa has been and continues to be one of the most sadistic and unforgivable crimes against humanity! From the rape of slaves owned by old dishonest George Washington, *{see: Hirschfeld, Fritz (1997). George Washington and Slavery. University of Missouri Press, p. 11; also: Number of slaves: Henry Wiencek, An Imperfect God: George Washington, His Slaves, and the Creation of America, p. 46}* to the participation of the U.S. - as an observer - at the infamous and divisive Berlin Conference of 1884-85. *See: How Oil Put Africa Back on the Map, by Ebere Onwudiwe }*, to the hundred years of lynching's during the reconstruction period after the American Civil War, to the Jim Crow legislation, segregation and institutionalized apartheid of the 1940's and 1960's, to the cruel castration of the anti-nationalist-integrationist-tokenism and cointelpro repression of the nineteen-seventies and eighties and right up to the current neo-liberal subterfuge and deception of the smiling face Obama drama strategy, the racist American capitalist system has been the arch enemy of African people and the masses of humanity!

Modern capitalism has grown out of a horrid history and legacy of cultural disrespect, greed, racism, oppression, exploitation, conquest, invasion and a barbarism unmatched in the sordid history of tyranny and anti-people State sponsor terror. While modern capitalism has accelerated technology to amazing heights, it has corrupted itself and morally degraded itself to the slime of the most depraved toxic swamp. America is the most technologically advance society in the world today and at the same time the most politically backward society in the world today. Its insanity clearly is in the fact that it feeds on itself and will sell to itself the noose that will be used to hang itself. Historically oppressive empires try to give the impression that they are invulnerable and that their power is uncontestable. Yet, history shows clearly that empires come and go, rise and fall and are eventually brought down by their own evil endeavors, along with the triumphant struggles of those whom they have oppressed. Martin L. King would never tire of saying, "The moral arm of the universe is long but it bends towards justice." History also shows that when oppressive empires fall, they disintegrate astonishingly quick! The American capitalist empire will be no exception to this historical maxim. Not even technologically advanced and "sophisticate" America will be able to avoid its' destiny with history. Those of us who are living in 2009 will witness the first major tumbling of the pillars of American capitalism and imperialism. The political-economic crisis, which currently is strangling all capitalist nations, and the present crisis in the international situation foretells the requiem that will surely befall the American government and its economy of doom. The "justice" forces of history will reclaim history, soon and very soon!

The current international financial and political situation of world capitalism is characterized by a large quantity of destabilization, political-economic uncertainty, military expansion and at the same time military defeat and setbacks, a rising world condemnation and isolation, a growing anti-war movement within America and around the world, a decomposition of the so-called "anti-terror coalition" organized by America, a ground swelling distrust of the American ruling class, devastating setbacks in Afghanistan and Iraq, a razor-sharp growth of mass revolutionary movements in Africa and throughout the Caribbean and Latin America, the growth of an American police state, a critical rising unemployment rate of over 10% which is a crisis in the communities of color within America, a deteriorating heath situation among the American citizenry – particularly in the communities of color, the beginnings of a anti-racist, anti-capitalist African and Latino youth movement in the U.S., American military intervention around the world which attacks popular governments around the world, neo-liberal and neo-fascist policies and an intensification of race-class struggle Things are not going well for American capitalism, in fact nothing is going right or well for them, and this situation only increases geometrically for the enemy of the peoples of the world. **"CHICKENS**

WILL COME HOME TO "ROOST". At the very moment that American capitalism appears to be resilient, at the very moment that the oppressors gives the false impression of permanency and being at their zenith, at the time that international finance capitalism manipulates its media and bourgeois scholars to portray a rose-colored picture of stability and growth, imperialism is entering its decisive period of decline, and empires fall quickly.

The global reach of the United States is backed by its' foreign policy by which the United States interacts with foreign nations. U.S. foreign policy from 1776 to present, in general - and specifically in relation to Africa - has been a policy and strategy of invasions, destabilizations, assassinations, State sponsored terror, deception, orchestrated coups, media, NGO and organizational manipulation, and a forked tong diplomacy, backed by a gun boat-air assault and infantry perverse persuasion financed by an over 13 trillion dollar economy and The new mouth of U.S. imperialism, - **Obama -** is seeking to increase the military budget as he calls for billions more to bail out the super-rich!

The officially stated goals of the foreign policy of the U.S. , as mentioned in the *Foreign Policy Agenda* of the U.S. Dept. of State , are "to create a more secure, democratic, and prosperous world for the benefit of the American people and the international community." *{U.S. Dept. of State - Foreign Policy Agenda}* **Nothing can be further from the truth!** *{The Enemy, What Every American Should Know About American Imperialism, By Felix Green* In addition, the U.S. House Committee on Foreign states as some of its jurisdictional goals: "export controls, including nonproliferation of nuclear technology and nuclear hardware; measures to foster commercial intercourse with foreign nations and to safeguard American business abroad. If America – that is the American ruling class – interest is capitalist development and expansion – **AND IT SURELY IS** – then America is about the business of exploitation and domination.

The foreign policy of the U.S., will only follow the path of the treacherous legacy that birthed this country, a tale of genocidal assault on the indigenous of the Western hemisphere, the oppressive utilization of Asian labor, the exploitation of White workers, and the enslavement of the African. **YOU CAN NOT BE A GOOD PRESIDENT OF AN EVIL EMPIRE!**

AN OVERVIEW OF US FOREIGN POLICY

THE ATTACK ON PEOPLE'S SOVERIGNITY

Quite obviously, all U.S. presidents since old dishonest George to "skinning-grinning" Obama have proudly endorse and attempted to rationalize and justify U.S. foreign policy. But, an accurate and objective analysis of U.S. history and international relations squarely places the U.S. at the top of evil empires! The record speaks for itself: *the bourgeoisie American revolution, the Spanish American war, the so-called Indian wars against the indigenous of the Western hemisphere – including the genocidal " Long march" in which over 16000 Cherokee began the* long march*, with one quarter to half dying along the way, the invasion of Africa by way of the Barbary Coast War, the war with British capitalism - called the War of 1812, the racist and expansionist Monroe Doctrine, the Roosevelt Corollary, the racist-fascist annexation of the Panama Canal, the expansion of the Rockefeller oil interest throughout Latin America, World War One and Two, the Korean War, the Truman Doctrine, the U.S. marine invasion of Trinidad, the Bay of Pigs Invasion, the invasion of Grenada, the Viet Nam War, the wars with Iraq and Afghanistan, the proxy wars and U.S. supplied and financed armies in Africa and Latin America, The U.S. sponsored invasion of Syria, the numerous CIA sponsored assassinations, the overthrow of Allende in Chili, the overthrown of Nkrumah in Ghana, the overthrow and assassination of Patrice Lumumba in the Congo, the thirty five U.S. backed successful assassinations that led to a regime changes- not counting the assassinations that did not lead to a regime change, the 737 U.S. military bases around the world that aid the U.S. in the control of* humanity's economic, social and political activities under the helm of U.S. corporate and military power. *and the continued policy of imperialist expansion and war that is endorsed by the Obama* *administration, all give repugnant testimony to the foreign policy record of the United Snakes!*

" Fret not thyself of evil doers, neither thou be envious against the workers of Iniquity. For hey shall soon be cut down like the grass and wither away." Psalms 37:1-2

In his *"A Brief History of U.S. Interventions: 1945 to the Present,"* William Blum, very convincingly argues: "The engine of American foreign policy has been fueled not by a devotion to any kind of morality, but rather by the necessity to serve other imperatives, which can be summarized as follows: * making the world safe for American corporations *enhancing the financial statements of defense contractors at home who have contributed generously to members of congress* preventing the rise of any society that might serve as a successful example of an alternative to the capitalist mode* extending political and economic hegemony over as wide an area as possible, as befits a "great power.* This in the name of fighting a supposed moral crusade against what cold warriors convinced themselves, and the American people, was the existence of an evil International Communist Conspiracy, which in fact never existed, evil or not." All the U.S. wars and related foreign policy actions of the US have never served the interest of the masses of the people in the U.S., although the masses havc died for what they confusingly thought was an effort to make the world safe and preserve democracy. But only the blind and unconscious do not see; for lack of vision the masses do die and suffer and will continue to do so if they do not gain consciousness. *{The Enemy, What Every American Should Know About American Imperialism, By Felix Green}* The ruling classes of U.S. capitalism have no morally social concern for the people of America or the world! For the ruling class, the interest of the people is not even the last concern. They despise the people; in the minds of the ruling class - with regards to the masses "there's not to reason why; there's only to consume, pay taxes, be exploited, fight and die!" With a deceptive smile on his face, Obama encourages the people to admit their faults, sacrifice and charge forward, while the conscious say, **"HELL NO! SAVE THE DRAMA FOR OBAMA'S MOMMA!"**

An Obama presidency would further legitimize and faultily justify the imperialist orientation and racist intent of U.S. foreign policy by inscribing it as liberalism or the "new kind" of progressivism.

"There's not to reason why; there's only to consume, pay taxes, be exploited, fight and die!"

A CONTINUATION OF NEO-LIBERAL EMPIRE BUILDING UNDER THE DISGUISE OF: Democracy { Demon- narcracy }

"Neo-liberalism" is a set of economic policies that have become widespread during the last 25 years or so. Although the word is rarely heard in the United States, you can clearly see the effects of neo-liberalism here as the rich grow richer and the poor grow poorer." {*What is "Neo-Liberalism"? A Brief Definition by Elizabeth Martinez and Arnoldo García*} For the understanding of this writing, a bit more can be added to the conscious description of Martinez and García.

Neo-liberalism - similar to neo-colonialism - is an imperialist strategy to hold and/ or expand the immoral and empire predation, annexation, and seizure of people's land. It is empire building with a deceptive title but imperial seizure nevertheless. According to Martinez and García, the main points of neo-liberalism include:

1. ***THE RULE OF THE MARKET***. Liberating "free" enterprise or private enterprise from any bonds imposed by the government (the state) no matter how much social damage this causes. Greater openness to international trade and investment, as in NAFTA. Reduce wages by de-unionizing workers and eliminating workers' rights that had been won over many years of struggle. No more price controls. All in all, total freedom of movement for capital, goods and services. To convince us this is good for us, they say "an unregulated market is the best way to increase economic growth, which will ultimately benefit everyone." It's like Reagan's "supply-

side" and "trickle-down" economics -- but somehow the wealth didn't trickle down very much.

2. ***CUTTING PUBLIC EXPENDITURE FOR SOCIAL SERVICES*** like education and health care. ***REDUCING THE SAFETY-NET FOR THE POOR***, and even maintenance of roads, bridges, water supply -- again in the name of reducing government's role. Of course, they don't oppose government subsidies and tax benefits for business.

3. ***DEREGULATION***. Reduce government regulation of everything that could diminish profits, including protecting the environment and safety on the job.

4. ***PRIVATIZATION***. Sell state-owned enterprises, goods and services to private investors. This includes banks, key industries, railroads, toll highways, electricity, schools, hospitals and even fresh water. Although usually done in the name of greater efficiency, which is often needed, privatization has mainly had the effect of concentrating wealth even more in *a few hands and making the public pay even more for its needs.*

5. ***ELIMINATING THE CONCEPT OF "THE PUBLIC GOOD" or "COMMUNITY"*** and replacing it with "individual responsibility." Pressuring the poorest people in a society to find solutions to their lack of health care, education and social security all by themselves -- then blaming them, if they fail, as "lazy." {*What is "Neo-Liberalism"? A Brief Definition* by Elizabeth Martinez and Arnoldo García}

In the United States, neo-liberalism is destroying welfare programs; attacking the rights of labor (including all immigrant workers); and cutting back social programs. The Republican "Contract" on America is pure neo-liberalism. Its supporters are working hard to deny protection to children, youth, women, the planet itself -- and trying to trick us into acceptance by saying this will "get government off my back." The beneficiaries of neo-liberalism are a minority of the world's people. For the vast majority it brings even more suffering than before:, suffering without end. **The Obama presidency is a neo-liberal strategy of deception!**

All forms of imperial territorial control and subjugation are **{ essentially colonialism }!** Weather you call it neo-liberalism, neo-colonialism, cultural domination, etc., all imperial territorial control and subjugation seeks to dominate and ideologically penetrate the minds, cultures, institutions and lands of a people. And, all oppression leads to the underdevelopment and demise of the subject people. Essentially, the oppressive State and its apparatus uses all at its means to further the interest and benefit of the oppressor. This *predator-victim relationship of imperialism*, manifest - by way of political domination - in the social, psychological, educational, economic, law enforcement and military realms. *{See: Towards Colonial Freedom, by Kwame Nkrumah}* The lives and neighborhoods of the oppressed are a very different place than that of the oppressor*{Franz Fanon, The Wretched of the Earth, and see, A Dying Colonialism}* The health, educational, cultural concerns and the indisputable human rights of the oppressed are absent! *Compassion is a vacuum in the minds and souls of the oppressor! But when the oppress do take on freedom, <u>they will do so without pity and without mercy!</u>*

Hypocritical insensitivity is the template of U.S. foreign policy and is clearly reflected in the contradiction between the aims of U.S. foreign policy and the lack of **social needs** and **humanitarian development**, the latter two being hallmarks of a genuine civilization. *{See: http://www.thirdworldtraveler.com/ link; U.S.Foreign Policy and Pentagon}*

With a smiling face of deception - media made Obama - took the occasion of his first press appearance as president-elect to declare his determination to impose policies of budgetary austerity to contend with a federal deficit for the current fiscal year which, according the Congressional Budget Office, is exceeding $10.7 trillion. Voicing the neo-liberal interest of the American ruling class and the **"not so hidden hand of Zionism"** that steers U.S. domestic and foreign policy, <u>Obama made clear the intent to eliminate many social programs, and by so doing discount the mass surge of the sixties and early seventies that</u>

forced the federal government to implement such reforms. The *"smiling face"* also declared his intent on cost-cutting in the entitlement programs such as Social Security, Medicare and Medicaid, callously ignoring the vital importance of such programs to tens of millions of elderly and poor people – with a triple devastating effect on people of color. Out of $10.7 trillion in total federal debt, about 40 percent, or $4.3 trillion, is borrowed from Social Security. The Trust Fund is the largest holder of federal debt, followed by US private investors, who hold $3.4 trillion, and foreign investors, many of them governments, who hold $3 trillion. Obama is willing to steal more from the poor to make the superrich, even richer. "The CBO figure of $1.2 trillion likely underestimates the current year's deficit by a significant amount. It includes nothing for the stimulus package which has yet to be spelled out in detail by the incoming administration, and assumes no emergency spending to finance Obama's promised buildup of US military forces in Afghanistan. Reuters reported Wednesday that Obama's secretary of defense, Robert Gates, a holdover from the Bush administration, is requesting an additional $70 billion for the ongoing wars in Iraq and Afghanistan, not counting the additional cost of a doubling of US forces to some 60,000 in Afghanistan.

Manipulating, redirecting, marginalizing, stealing, and maliciously misappropriating the wealth of its mass citizenry in order to accumulate more power, wealth and unjust-capital is *business as usual* for empires. It was done in the imperial conquest of Rome, Persia, Gangues Khan, Spain, Britain, Germany, Russia, and China and with the current most powerful empire in human history, the united snakes of amerikkka. Yet, when empires fall they collapse astonishingly quick, the results of an internal and external moral, social, political ideological, and economic malignancy that is a characteristic pathology of systemic evil and injustice – **YOU REAP WHAT YOU SOW AND THE EVIL YOU DO WILL SURELY RETUN UNTO YOUR OWN HOUSE!** The

indicators below are just a small list of evidence that the crisis of capitalism and US domestic and foreign policy **is just beginning!**

Chapter Four   Betrayal: A Litany of Deception, Lies and Hypocrisy

Five years after the election of Barak Obama - *the black ace card of the American racist-ruling class* - we can look back at a telling track record and we see a train wreck of broken promises and dashed hopes on the part of millions. The economy, in realty, is in dismay and rapidly approaching depression and devastation. Unemployment is off the chain and millions have simply stopped looking for work. Consumer self-assurance is demoralized, although the coffers of the rich are overflowing! The U.S. involvement in foreign wars *for over thirteen years* has shattered many in the armed forces which now has a suicide rate greater than any other army in the world as the U.S. pursues an uncertain foreign strategy of anxiety and desperation. *Of course, Barak Obama cannot be blamed for all this, for he is just the U.S. president - an office whose primary responsibility is to be a face to a naive and mostly unconscious public and a mouthpiece for the American racist-ruling class!*

> Out of hundreds of broken promises,
>
> the list below is 42 of the most blatant betrayals[3]

1. Barack Obama repeatedly made the promise that "you will be able to keep your health care plan" under Obamacare.
2. "If you like your doctor, you will be able to keep your doctor
3. "My administration is committed to creating an unprecedented level of openness in government."

➤ [3] PolitiFact -- the Pulitzer Prize-winning project of the Tampa Bay Times that has essentially tracked all of the president's major promises -- ruled Obama's argument "mostly false."

➤ The project finds that Obama has kept 241, or 45 percent, of his roughly 500 campaign promises, while breaking 118, or 22 percent, and compromising on roughly 25 percent. The remaining 8 percent are essentially still to be determined

4. "We agree on reforms that will finally reduce the costs of health care. Families will save on their premiums..."

5. "We've got shovel-ready projects all across the country that governors and mayors are pleading to fund. And the minute we can get those investments to the state level, jobs are going to be created."

6. "And we will pursue the housing plan I'm outlining today. And through this plan, we will help between 7 and 9 million families restructure or refinance their mortgages so they can afford—avoid foreclosure."

7. "I will sign a universal health-care bill into law by the end of my first term as president that will cover every American and cut the cost of a typical family's premium by up to $2,500 a year."

8. "We reject the use of national security letters to spy on citizens who are not suspected of a crime."

9. "We will close the detention camp in Guantanamo Bay, the location of so many of the worst constitutional abuses in recent years."

10. "Allow Americans to buy their medicines from other developed countries if the drugs are safe and prices are lower outside the U.S."

11. "We will revisit the Patriot Act and overturn unconstitutional

12. "Will ensure that federal contracts over $25,000 are competitively bid."

13. We reject sweeping claims of 'inherent' presidential power."

14. Will eliminate all income taxation of seniors making less than $50,000 per year. This will eliminate taxes for 7 million seniors — saving them an average of $1,400 a year– and will also mean that 27 million seniors will not need to file an income tax return at all."

15. "We support constitutional protections and judicial oversight on any surveillance program involving Americans."

16. "If we have not gotten our troops out by the time I am president, it is the first thing I will do. I will get our troops home, we will end this war. You can take that to the bank."

17. "Will not sign any non-emergency bill without giving the American public an opportunity to review and comment on the White House website for five days."

18. "The President does not have power under the Constitution to unilaterally authorize a military attack in a situation that does not involve stopping an actual or imminent threat to the nation."
19. I'm pledging to cut the deficit we inherited in half by the end of my first term in office. This will not be easy. It will require us to make difficult decisions and face challenges we've long neglected. But I refuse to leave our children with a debt that they cannot repay – and that means taking responsibility right now, in this administration, for getting our spending under control."
20. The project also concludes Obama's promise to create 5 million new "green" jobs also is still in the works.
21. Eliminate all oil and gas tax loopholes
22. End income tax for seniors making less than $50,000
23. Create a $60 billion bank to fund roads and bridges
24. Sign the Employee Free Choice Act, making it easier for workers to unionize
25. Forbid companies in bankruptcy from giving executives bonuses
26. Forbid companies in bankruptcy from giving executives bonuses
27. Allow imported prescription drugs
28. Prevent drug companies from blocking generic drugs
29. Double federal funding for cancer research
30. Require employers to provide seven paid sick days per year
31. Reduce the Veterans Benefits Administration claims backlog
32. Form international group to help Iraq refugees
33. Restore habeas corpus rights for "enemy combatants"
34. Seek independent watchdog agency to investigate congressional ethics violations
35. Allow five days of public comment before signing bills
36. Double funding for afterschool programs
37. "Will create new Teacher Service Scholarships that will cover four years of undergraduate or two years of graduate teacher education, including high-quality alternative programs for mid-career recruits in exchange for teaching for at least four years in a high-need field or location."

38. Sign the Deceptive Practices and Voter Intimidation Prevention Act into law

39. Sign the Deceptive Practices and Voter Intimidation Prevention Act into law

40. Increase the supply of affordable housing throughout metropolitan regions

41. Increase the minimum wage to $9.50 an hour

42. Restore Superfund program so that polluters pay for clean-ups

BROKEN PROMISES Healthcare:

Beware - Obamacare Will Not Provide!

It will make the rich, richer and further degrade the conditions of most!

The gullibility, unconsciousness, and confusion of most in America will be taken advantage of *"once again"* by the racist-ruling class via the Obama administration! This time, it is by the deceptive and anti-humanitarian legislation and pathological policies of the Patient Protection and Affordable Care Act (ACA*) - It will make the rich, richer and further degrade the conditions of most!* After years of promotion, and political power struggle, health insurance exchanges are opening for "profitable" business across the country as part of the Patient Protection and Affordable Care Act (ACA). Under the masquerade of a health care renovation, people without health insurance are mandated to purchase coverage from private insurers or face a penalty. Coverage for enrollees set to begin January 1, 2014. In the guise of "reform," insurance exchanges will receive billions of dollars into their coffers along with slashing costs for the government and corporations.

In his bid for the presidency, Barack Obama promised to implement a sweeping social reform in the provision of health care in the United States. He claimed that under his plan, "no insurer would be allowed to deny coverage to a sick child, or an individual with a preexisting condition; no family would go bankrupt or hungry due to health care costs; and that the insurance companies would be held to account." A colossal fraud has been perpetrated against the American population in the name of Obamacare, and that all of these promises were lies. After the bill's passage, one concession after another was made to big business: only companies with 50 or more employees would have to provide insurance, only those working 30 hours or more had to be covered. Feeble plans without hospitalization and surgery coverage would be considered "adequate" employee-sponsored plans. Those businesses that do not comply would only face token penalties. People without coverage through their employer, or from a government program such as Medicare or Medicaid, are to make up the fresh pool of captive, cash-paying customers who must fend for themselves on the insurance exchanges. One common feature among the confusing array of plans is the alarming reality that the least expensive plans offer the lowest levels of coverage with limited choices, and the highest out-of-pocket costs.

Focus will be on the following aspects of Obamacar: **Austerity** deep cutbacks in Social Security and Medicaid - **State responsibility and employers - Big business and the private insurers -Technical glitches and mandatory computer chip implants - The race/class issues** and millions of people living in poverty - **REAL SOLUTIONS**

Austerity- Deep Cutbacks in Social Security and Medicaid:

The working class and the poor in many European cities can testify that austerity is a term that describes sever cutbacks in government revenue formerly allocated or legislated for those in need. The masses of Europe are in uproar and militant protest against their governments and view **austerity as a fascist policy against the poor to protect and promote the interest of the rich!** In the U.S., two-face legislators and system media, avoid using the term austerity, and seek to deceive under names such as: fiscal cliff, sequestration and Govt. shutdown – *oppression by any other name, is still oppression!* The mass response to recent {American austerity} will lead to not only mass protest, but mass resistance and rebellion in 2014!

In a White House statement, President Obama made clear that he would push for new cuts in social programs, leading to major attacks on the core programs for retirees dating from the New Deal and the Great Society--Medicare and Social Security. "The key now is a budget that cuts out the things that we don't need," Obama said, adding, "The challenges we have right now are not short-term deficits; it's the long-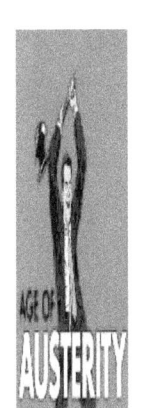term obligations around things like Medicare and Social Security." White House Press Secretary Jay Carney - hiding behind the deceptive statement - "bipartisan compromise" and the search for "common ground", noted that the budget proposal Obama submitted earlier this year made **"tough choices"** toward "further reducing our deficit." The phrase "tough choices" is a Washington euphemism for unprecedented attacks on social program on which tens of millions of working people rely. On health care, the Democratic Senate budget proposes $275 billion in cuts, mostly to Medicare providers. The House budget, drafted by Congressman Ryan, proposes $2.7 trillion in cuts, including a repeal of Obama's health care overhaul, massive cuts in the Medicaid government health insurance program for the poor, and the transformation of Medicare into a privatized voucher system. Obama is meanwhile pushing for a huge cut in corporate taxes as part of a long-term budget deal.

According to the Pan-African News Wire {Abayomi Azikiwe Editor} "Massive cuts are being proposed which will impact the way in which Social Security and Medicaid are allocated in the United States. The Obama administration has floated a plan known as chained Consumer Price Index (CPI) along with a goal of trimming healthcare funding for the poor and elderly by $400 billion. In a recent study released by the Center for Global Policy Solutions (CGPS), the research institute placed the Obama administration proposals within a broader sociological context where the historic national oppression of African in Americans has rendered this community to lower-wages and accumulated household wealth. Compounding this centuries-old reality, the economic crisis of the last five years has also disproportionately driven down the living standards of African Americans and other peoples of color. With specific reference to Medicaid, the Joint Center for Economic and Political Studies (JCEPS) wrote over a year ago that reductions in funding for this program would cause tremendous suffering among the Africanin American and Latino populations. The same research institute argues that these cuts would in fact increase costs for healthcare companies since people would still need care whether it is funded by the government or not."

There is nothing progressive in the Obamacare legislation; Obama's policies towards the majority have consistently been geared toward *increasing* advantages for the rich ad increasing social inequality for the mass! The claim that the health care overhaul is an oasis of progress in this desert of social reaction is simply a lie. These words Social inequality has now reached levels not seen in nearly a century, and official poverty levels have risen to a near-generation high of 15 percent, with more than 46 million Americans impoverished, an in communities of color , the situation is geometrically worse!

People without coverage through their employer, or from a government program such as Medicare or Medicaid, are to make up the fresh pool of captive, cash-paying customers who must fend for themselves on the insurance exchanges. According to the Congressional Budget Office, the health care overhaul will leave an estimated 31 million people—about a tenth of the US population—uninsured by 2023. Undocumented workers and their families are barred from purchasing coverage on the exchanges. Due to a "family glitch" in the law, businesses are only required to provide "affordable" insurance to their employees, not to their employees' families, so those family members will not receive subsidies to purchase coverage on the exchanges. The very poorest people will also be ineligible in some states. While the US Supreme Court ruled the ACA constitutional, it struck down a component of the law that called for expanding Medicaid. The result is that in 21 states, many people making below the poverty level will not be eligible for either ACA subsidies or Medicaid. Still others will be forced to go without coverage because they simply cannot afford it, with or without the government subsidies.

State Responsibility and Employers

The oppressed cannot look to their oppressors to solve the problems of their oppression. Now more than half of the 50 U.S. states are opting out of Medicaid xpansion which would have provided health care coverage for adults making up to 133 percent of the poverty level. This means **the very poorest of the uninsured—those with annual incomes between 32 percent and 100 percent of the poverty level ($6,250-$19,530)**—will have no affordable health care options. They will be eligible for neither Medicaid nor subsidies to purchase coverage on the exchanges, which are only available for people from the poverty level to four times that rate – Obamacare will not provide for them. Moreover, benefit payments from the U.S. government's Supplemental Nutrition Assistance Program (SNAP), better known as food stamps, will be slashed drastically on November 1, the first across-the-board cut in food stamp benefits in U.S. history. The cuts will amount to $5 billion per year, and a total of $11 billion through 2016. The average household of three will receive a benefit cut of $29 a month, or $319 per year.

A gigantic number of people work for employers with less than fifty employees. The law requires companies with 50 or more employees to provide affordable insurance to their workers or be penalized with an excise tax. However, these businesses are not required to offer coverage to employees who work less than 30 hours a week; consequently, many will be laid off or have work hours drastically cut, forcing them into - no health care coverage. Obamacare was never meant for the poor, in reality , it is a loop whole for the rich! Small businesses are cutting back on hiring to avoid crossing the 50-employee threshold defining a large business, thus avoiding the requirement that they offer insurance. Still other businesses are considering ditching their health care altogether and paying the federal penalty instead, which in a considerable number of cases would be to the companies' economic advantage.

Even in those companies with 50 workers or more, a loophole in the ACA will allow these businesses to offer bare bone insurance plans and still meet the law's requirements. These "skinny plans"—costing employers as little as $40 to $100 a month per employee—may cover minimal requirements such as preventive services, but offer no coverage for hospitalizations or surgeries. For thousands of workers and their dependents with serious medical situations – this will mean bankruptcy and destitution.

Big business is seizing on the ACA to shift retirees and active workers to private insurance exchanges, where the burden of inadequate care will be placed on them. In place of employer-administered health plans, these workers will receive a health care stipend that they can use to purchase coverage on a private insurance exchange where rates will inevitably increase dramatically – under capitalism, the major focus of business is profit , not humanitarian concerns, and certainly not good health! Companies employing tens of thousands of workers are making this move. Among others, IBM and Time Warner are shifting retirees to private exchanges, while Walgreens, Sears Holding, and Darden Restaurants are moving all active employees off their company-administered health plans to these exchanges. State and local governments are abandoning thousands and seeking to trim health care costs by dumping active and retired workers onto the government-sponsored health care exchanges as well. The City of Detroit, which has filed for bankruptcy, aims to drastically reduce the $5.7 billion owed to retirees in health benefits by pushing those 65 and older onto Medicare and dumping those too young to qualify for the government-run program onto the ACA insurance markets.

Big business and the private insurers have *"shamefully and successfully"* lobbied the Obama administration to remove any token regulations contained in the legislation that might impede their profits. This past July, the White House announced that it would be delaying by one year an ACA requirement that businesses with 50 or more employees provide insurance to those working 30 hours a week or more. Companies will not be fined the $2,000 stipulated in the bill for failure to provide this coverage. Meanwhile the "individual mandate," which requires those without insurance to obtain coverage or pay a fine, remains in place. And last month, the president ditched another so-called consumer protection provision of the legislation, granting a one-year grace period for insurers to adhere to limits on out-of-pocket health care costs. Obama—who touted this cap on costs as a protection for families against bankruptcy due to a catastrophic medical condition, or the high cost of certain treatments and drugs—will allow insurers to continue to gouge the insured to the tune of tens of thousands of dollars.

The oppressed cannot look to their oppressors to solve the problems of their oppression.

A largely undetected loophole in the ACA rules came to light indicating that some larger employers will be able to provide bare-bones coverage that offers minimal requirements such as preventive services,  but may not provide coverage for surgeries, hospital stays, or other vital services. Companies providing these "skinny plans" will be able to dodge the $2,000 per worker penalties for failure to provide adequate and affordable coverage. A cornerstone of the health care overhaul is the gutting of Medicare, which serves an estimated 50 million seniors. The bill proposes a $700 billion cut to the government-run program over 10 years. Doctors have already begun to limit the number of Medicare patients they treat or drop them altogether as the ACA takes aim at the fee-for-service system and imposes new evaluation and payment procedures for Medicare doctors aimed at eliminating "unnecessary" tests and procedures. Despite promises that the health care bill would provide "near universal coverage," the Congressional Budget Office predicted earlier this year that 30 million people will remain uninsured two years into the legislation, in 2016. Many more will be underinsured, either due to cutbacks through their employer-sponsored plans or their inability to purchase anything but the cheapest, inferior plans on the government-run health care exchanges.

States that are not expanding Medicaid

According to the Congressional Budget Office (CBO), the 31 million uninsured people will include those left out because their resident states are not expanding Medicaid, those excluded because they are undocumented immigrants, those who cannot receive ACA subsidies due to a "family glitch" related to employer coverage, and those who choose not to purchase coverage because they cannot afford it.

A large proportion of those projected to remain insured are very poor people living in states that are not expanding Medicaid to cover them. The .U.S Supreme Court ruled the ACA constitutional in June 2012, but also ruled that states could not be mandated to comply with a provision of the law that would extend Medicaid to those currently not covered in many states.

The ACA provides subsidies to purchase insurance for individuals and families whose incomes are between 100 percent and 400 percent of the federal poverty level on a sliding scale. It was assumed that those below this level would be covered by Medicaid. But without the Medicaid expansion in many states, some of the poorest people will be left out in the cold.

In Virginia, a state that has chosen not to expand its Medicaid program, a single, childless man making below the official poverty level—an abysmal $11,490 for an individual in 2013—will not qualify for Medicaid because Virginia offers the program only to single, childless men if they are disabled.

A recent *New York Times* analysis of U.S. Census data found that two-thirds of single mothers and poor African Americans and half of the low-wage workers who are currently uninsured will be left without coverage due to the effect of this Medicaid no-man's land. About two-thirds of the nation's poor uninsured African Americans and single mothers, and about 60 percent of the uninsured working poor, live in the 26 states that are not planning to expand Medicaid. The 26 states not expanding Medicaid—mainly located in the Deep South and Mountain West, and predominantly Republican ruled—are citing the funding mechanism under the ACA to justify their decision not to expand the program for the poor. The ACA stipulates that the federal government will cover 100 percent of the costs for the first three years, drop to 95 percent in 2017, and remain at 90 percent after 2020. The state governments argue that they cannot afford any percentage of the expansion costs.

Even after the bill's passage, without the much-vaunted "public option," one **concession after another was made to big business**: only companies with 50 or more employees would have to provide insurance, only those working 30 hours or more had to be covered. Bare-bones, "skinny" plans—without hospitalization and surgery coverage—would be considered "adequate" employee-sponsored plans. Those businesses that do not comply would face minimal penalties. People without coverage through their employer, or from a government program such as Medicare or Medicaid, are to make up the fresh pool of captive, cash-paying customers who must fend for themselves on the insurance exchanges. Beginning today, those browsing the offerings on the new "marketplace" will confront a confusing array of plans, but with one common feature: 7/ least expensive plans offer the lowest levels of coverage with limited choices, and the highest out-of-pocket costs.

While those shopping for insurance plans will be provided with minimal government stipends or none at all, **8/there is no meaningful oversight over what the insurance companies can charge for coverage**. If an insufficient number of young, healthy people sign up, the insurers can be expected to jack up premiums even higher to bolster their cash flow.[i]

Big Business and the Private Insurers

The health care exchanges, set up for adults under 65 and their dependents, are required to open for enrollment by October 1, 2013 with the insurance provided through them set to begin January 2014. Individuals and families who do not receive "affordable" insurance through their employer, or through a government program such as Medicaid, will be required to purchase coverage through private insurers via these marketplaces or pay a penalty, receiving modest government subsidies to do so.

The first of these exchanges first of these exchanges has already gone into effect in California. Insurer Blue Shield of California has projected that it will increase premiums by an average of 13 percent in the first year alone. But as the health care law goes into effect across the country, premiums can be expected to rise at an even more rapid pace *– in the U.S., profits supersede healthcare!*

A recent report by the U.S. House Committee on Energy and Commerce found that individuals in about 90 % of U.S. states would likely face **"significant premium increases."** Based on responses from 17 insurance companies, the report estimates that individuals purchasing coverage on the individual market could face average premium increases of nearly 100 percent, with potential increases of 400 percent *– in the U.S., profits supersede healthcare!* Insurers offering coverage on the exchanges are required to cover a standard set of benefits, including prescription drugs, maternity and preventative care. They cannot turn away people with pre-existing conditions or charge older customers more for coverage. Limits on maximum co-payments and other out-of-pocket costs, on the other hand, are high: $6,400 a year for individuals and $12,500 for families. However, insurers are hiking premiums to make up for any increased costs resulting from offering the ACA-specified coverage on the individual market. Despite a rule in the federal law that requires review of any requests for more than a 10 percent increase in premiums, there are wide disparities in how the review process operates at the state level.

A new survey by InsuranceQuotes.com show that two-thirds of Americans who are currently uninsured are undecided whether they will purchase coverage by the January 1 deadline. These people will either be priced out of the market or will decide they are young and healthy enough to take the risk of going uninsured. Most will then have to pay the penalty for not obtaining insurance. If enough people opt out of the exchange market, the insurance companies can be expected to jack up prices even further.

As originally proposed by the Obama administration, about half of those presently uninsured were to gain coverage through an expansion of Medicaid, the health care program for the poor jointly administered by the federal government and the states. In its ruling upholding the ACA last June, the U.S. Supreme Court also ruled that states could not be required to expand their Medicaid programs. Now more than half of the 50 US states are opting out of the Medicaid expansion, which would have provided health care coverage for adults making up to 133 percent of the poverty level. **This means that the very poorest of the uninsured—those with annual incomes between 32 percent and 100 percent of the poverty level ($6,250-$19,530)—will have no affordable health care options**. They will be eligible for neither Medicaid nor subsidies to purchase coverage on the exchanges, which are only available for people from the poverty level to four times that rate.

The law requires companies with 50 or more employees to provide affordable insurance to their workers or be penalized with an excise tax. However, these businesses are not required to offer coverage to employees who work less than 30 hours a week. Other small businesses are cutting back on hiring to avoid crossing the 50-employee threshold defining a large business, thus avoiding the requirement that they offer insurance. Still other businesses are considering ditching their health care altogether and paying the federal penalty instead, which in a considerable number of cases would be to the companies' economic advantage. Even in those companies with 50 workers or more, a loophole in the ACA will allow these businesses to offer bare-bones insurance plans and still meet the law's requirements. These "skinny plans"—costing employers as little as $40 to $100 a month per employee—may cover minimal requirements such as preventive services, but offer no coverage for hospitalizations or surgeries. For workers and their dependents with such plans, one serious medical event could spell bankruptcy and destitution.

Workers offered these plans would have the option of purchasing insurance on the exchanges. But for workers in retail and other low-wage sectors this coverage would be prohibitively expensive, even with subsidies. The Kaiser Family Foundation estimates that a full-time worker earning $9 an hour could have to pay as much as $70 a month to purchase a mid-level exchange plan President Obama speaking at a Maryland community college to promote his health care overhaul, claimed that many plans on the exchanges "will cost much less than they do now" because insurance companies will be competing for business – *in the U.S., profits supersede healthcare!* In reality, many uninsured people who begin to shop for health care coverage on the exchanges will be in for a rude shock. The preponderance of "affordable" coverage will consist of cut-rate plans that leave the insured responsible for a considerable proportion of the costs. Premiums will vary widely from state to state and many plans with lower premiums will significantly limit the choice of doctors and hospitals. With few exceptions, individuals and families that do not receive insurance through an employer or a government program such as Medicare or Medicaid will be required to obtain insurance or pay a fine.

All of the coverage is offered by private insurance companies that have tailored policies to suit their profit interests. They are banking on a substantial number of young, healthy people signing up for coverage to offset costs associated with requirements that sicker individuals or those with pre-existing conditions not be charged higher premiums or turned away. If adequate numbers of young and relatively healthy people do not sign up, premiums are sure to rise. According to figures provided by the Department of Health and Human Services (HHS), premiums for a mid-range "silver" plan will average $328 a month nationally, before any tax credit subsidies are applied. But silver plan costs will vary greatly, ranging from a low of $172 in Minnesota to a high of $516 in Wyoming. The same plan will cost $373 in California, $328 in Florida, and $305 in Texas.

The health care overhaul is affecting a shift in the insurance market as a whole. Some companies and municipalities are already planning to end coverage for retirees and/or active workers, dumping them onto the exchanges. Still others are ending traditional employer coverage and offering workers a defined contribution to purchase coverage on private insurance "exchanges" set up by their employers, with limited choices and high out-of-pocket costs. One in four employers are reportedly considering moving their workers to a private exchange over the next three to five years. The health care bill is thus playing an additional insidious role, serving as a model for employers and local governments that currently provide insurance to an estimated 150 million people. Employer-sponsored insurance, which since World War II has been the traditional way workers at most companies received coverage, is being eliminated by many employers and replaced with a voucher system. The same type of sea-change is being eyed in relation to Medicare by politicians of both big business parties, who would like to see the government-run program for millions of seniors and the disabled scrapped in favor of a voucher system.

<u>Technical Glitches and</u> *Mandatory Computer Chip Implants*

A devastating and demoralizing start for

Obamacare health exchanges

On October 1,2013 the health insurance exchanges set up under the Obama administration's Patient Protection and Affordable Care Act (ACA) opened for business. Innumerable problems with the online marketplaces has been the results with tens of thousands of potential customers staring at locked screens, unable to enroll, or find out whether they qualify for government subsidies to purchase insurance. These computer failures are technical in nature; yet they reflect the social detach and social evasive nature of the entire Obamacare enterprise and the racist-ruling class that controls the office of the U.S. presidency . The first two weeks of a program that President Obama promised would vastly expand the availability of affordable health care to the 49 million Americans without health insurance have proven to be an absolute catastrophe. The most technologically advanced country in the world – a super power – that has the technical ability to tap the phones of presidents and every individual U.S. citizen; it can send spaceships to the edges of the galaxy, but cannot provide web service to a program that it promised would provide for the health of its' citizens!

More than $400 million was spent to design and implement the online exchanges, the majority of it going to private contractors. A report released by the Washington, DC-based nonprofit *Sunlight Foundation Reporting Group* reveals that these contractors were for the most part existing government contractors with "deep political pockets," including Northrop Grumman, General Dynamics, Deloitte, and Booz Allen Hamilton. According to the report: ***All but one of the 47 contractors who won contracts to carry out work on the Affordable Care Act worked for the government prior to its passage.*** The report noted that many played a major role in lobbying for the legislation, stating that ***some 17 contract winners reported spending more than $128 million on lobbying in 2011 and 2012.*** Why did they get the work? The report [produced by Sunlight Foundation Reporting Group, a Washington, D.C.-based nonprofit that focuses on government transparency] hints at a likely reason: The companies were big lobbyists, with "some 17 contract winners reported spending more than $128 million on lobbying in 2011 and 2012." Granted, some experience with government work is vital for any contractor, and the federal procurement system is geared to favor those already doing government work, but Sunlight pointed out that the list tips heavily toward those with both existing contracts and political leverage. The close collaboration of the government with these private companies is emblematic of the health care overhaul itself, which has never been about improving medical care or access for ordinary Americans, but rather about funneling billions of dollars into the coffers of the private health insurers and slashing costs for the government and corporations Obama's "ACA will in fact create a 'market.' But the market will be a federally controlled and federally regulated oligopoly. Government will also determine who is an authorized payer (only authorized insurers and the government itself through Medicare and Medicaid) and therefore limit 'demand.'"

The system's sustainability depends on getting enough healthy people to sign up, he pointed out, and if they don't then insurers "will have to raise everyone's premiums," which "could create what actuaries call a 'death spiral': Rising premiums prompt people to drop out, causing premiums to increase even more." Out of the fog surrounding the botching of HealthCare.gov appears the real reason for the crash and burn of the website in the microcosm and the ultimate failure of project Obamacare in the macrocosm: it will raise profits hand-over-fist for transnational insurance corporations. This is the reason Obamacare was created – not to take care of the health of the people, but to foist yet another fleecing upon them, one enforced at gunpoint by the IRS expropriation agency.

Chip Implants Mandatory

Most Americans won't like and probably won't believe that . ObamaCare has a microchip implant for you. The Obama Health care will includes - *under Class II, Paragraph 1, Section B) "(ii) a class II device that is implantable". Then on page 1004 it describes what the erm "data" means in paragraph 1, section B*:

(B) In this paragraph, the term 'data' refers to information respecting a device described in paragraph (1), including claims data, patient survey data, standardized analytic files that allow for the pooling and analysis of data from disparate data environments, electronic health records, and any other data deemed appropriate by the Secretary

As approved by the FDA, a class II implantable device is an "implantable radio frequency transponder system for patient

identification and health information. This sort of device would be implanted in the majority of people who opt to become covered by the public health care option. With the reform of the private insurance companies, many people will switch their coverage to a more affordable insurance plan. This means the number of people who choose the public option will increase. This also means the number of people chipped will be plentiful as well. The adults who choose to have a chip implanted are the lucky (yes, lucky) ones in this case. Children who are "born in the United States who at the time of birth is not otherwise covered under acceptable coverage" will be qualified and placed into the CHIP or Children's Health Insurance Program (what a convenient name). With a name like CHIP it would seem consistent to have the chip implanted into a child. Children conceived by parents who are already covered under the public option will more than likely be implanted with a chip by the consent of the parent. Eventually everyone will be implanted with a chip. *{See article in this edition - MICROCHIP IMPLANTS, MINDCONTROL AND CYBERNETICS}*

The Race/Class Issues and Millions of People Living in Poverty

The three quotes below are a good preface to shed light on the race/class nature of Obamacare

"Obama represents a sector or class of the Africans in the US that are hell bent on supporting the multinational class headed by the American ruling class, and Obama represents a sector or class benefiting from world imperialism and American capitalism; in fact, he represents the upper sectors of the African bourgeoisie. **Be not confused by this term bourgeoisie! Especially for the African, it is neither best defined nor understood by just a simple analysis of income, type of car, wealth, neighborhood and dress**. Such items are not the best indicators of the self-centered and anti-mass views that this class holds as mandatory tenets of its elitist ideology. However, this is not to say that all that are a part of this class are dedicated to its values. As Almical Cabral very clearly states. Some in the African bourgeoisie class have consciously decided to commit class suicide Obama represents a sector or class of the Africans in the US that are hell bent on supporting the multinational class headed by the American ruling class, and Obama represents a sector or class benefiting from world imperialism and American capitalism; in fact, he represents the upper sectors of the African bourgeoisie. **Be not confused by this term bourgeoisie! Especially for the African, it is neither best defined nor understood by just a simple analysis of income, type of car, wealth, neighborhood and dress**. Such items are not the best indicators of the self-centered and anti-mass views that this class holds as mandatory tenets of its elitist ideology. However, this is not to say that all that are a part of this class are dedicated to its values. As Almical Cabral very clearly states. Some in the African bourgeoisie class have consciously decided to commit class suicide." {*Gideon Odinga Mukhtar Obama Drama: A Strategy of Neo-Liberal Deception* – Listed on Amazon

"While racist social structure is not inherent in the colonial situation, it is inseparable from capitalist economic development. For race is inextricably linked with class exploitation; in a racist-capitalist power structure, capitalist exploitation and race oppression are complementary..." {*Kwame Nkrumah, Class Struggle in Africa*}

"Obama is the race card now being played on a neo-colonial level. Obama represents a strategy that seeks to blur and hide the reality of class antagonisms (inside and outside of the African context) and the racist policy of a capitalist ideology and stratagem, but this is consistent with neo-colonialism which seeks to hide the real hand of power, a power that is quite content on manipulation from real sources of power behind the façade of a Black, media made smiling face!" {*Ibid: Gideon Odinga Mukhtar Obama Drama: A Strategy of Neo-Liberal Deception*

Obamacare policies have been geared toward *increasing* social inequality… The claim that *the health care overhaul is an oasis of progress in this desert of social reaction* is simply a lie." Social inequality has now reached levels not seen in nearly a century, and official poverty levels have risen to a near-generation high of 15 percent, with more than 46 million Americans impoverished. This immense growth of social inequality and the domination of society and the political system by a financial aristocracy are incompatible with governmental claims of providing for the domestic welfare! The social reforms of the 1930s and 1960s, including Social Security and Medicare, won by previous generations of workers in bitter struggle, are in the sights of the ruling class austerity and targeted for ultimate destruction.

The poor and the majority of people of color will be forced to purchase their own insurance and will be particularly hard hit by premium costs. More than one-third of those with incomes below 133 percent of the federal poverty level spent 10 percent or more of their income on premium costs. Among those who must purchase their own coverage, 31 percent reported spending 10 percent or more of their income on premiums. Under the Obama health care overhaul, individuals and families will be required to obtain health care coverage or pay a penalty. Those who are not insured through their employer and are not eligible for government programs such as Medicaid will be required to purchase coverage on the insurance exchanges set up under the Affordable Care Act and may obtain subsidies to do so base on income. But this will not provide relief to the vast majority of those who are currently uninsured and underinsured. An article to be published this week in the ***Journal of General Internal Medicine*** notes that most low-income households, despite receiving subsidies, will be able to afford only the lowest-tier of health care on the exchanges, the so-called Bronze plans.

While someone making up to 133 percent of the federal poverty level will be required to pay only 2 percent of his or her income to obtain Bronze coverage, these inferior plans will cover only 60 percent of costs, leaving the insured with the responsibility to pick up the remaining 40 percent. This will inevitably lead to "insured" families skipping care, treatments and medications. Physicians for a National Health Program calculates that a 56-year-old making $45,900 will pay an estimated $4,361 in premiums for individual Bronze coverage, after subsidies, and up to $4,167 in additional deductibles and co-pays. This means that more than 18 percent of his or her income will go toward health care costs. **Obamacare,** far from guaranteeing decent medical care for all, will institutionalize inferior and inadequate care for tens of millions of Americans and lead to a reduction in coverage or an increase in costs for millions more who are currently covered under employer-sponsored plans. It will at the same time guarantee increased profits for the insurance industry by supplying it with millions of additional paying customers

The article below is very helpful in showing the Obamacare conditions and hypocrisy as it relates particularly to Africans in America {Black people}

"Massive cuts are being proposed which will impact the way in Social Security and Medicaid are allocated in the United States. The Obama administration has floated a plan known as chained Consumer Price Index (CPI) along with a goal of trimming healthcare funding for the poor and elderly by $400 billion. These efforts are purportedly connected with the need to trim the federal budget deficit. A "sequester" was imposed earlier this year which is already resulting in furloughs for government workers, lay-offs in the healthcare industry and the elimination of programs which have benefitted low-income people for decades. The chained CPI will lead to severe reductions of the limited increases in payments based upon the rise in inflation and the cost of living. These reforms, if instituted, would also be applied to benefits received by retired government employees, veterans and recipients of Supplemental Security Income (SSI).

In a recent study released by the Center for Global Policy Solutions (CGPS), the research institute placed the Obama administration proposals within a broader sociological context where the historic national oppression of African Americans has rendered this community to lower-wages and accumulated household wealth. Compounding this centuries-old reality, the economic crisis of the last five years has also disproportionately driven down the living standards of African Americans and other peoples of color. After retirement African Americans face even lower incomes through pensions and social security payments which are based on earnings during the last few years of their employment. Any cuts to the incremental increases in monthly payments for retirees can only result in deeper economic challenges and poverty. According to the CGPS study, "African Americans are among the most vulnerable when it comes to economic security. As of 2011, over hall of the African American senior population was financially insecure."

This financial insecurity stems from the continued lack of opportunity and systematic national discrimination within the education sector and labor market. In addition, the decades-long restructuring of the industrial and service sectors of the United States economy has left whole layers of the workforce without decent jobs that encompass adequate salaries and benefits. CGPS says that "The persistent income and wealth inequality seen among African Americans comes from years of disproportionately lower levels of earnings, employment, educational attainment, and ownership of family assets such as homes, stocks/bonds, saving accounts, and businesses. As a result, African Americans have had significantly fewer opportunities to build assets over time and often lack the savings to ensure financial security throughout their post-working years."

Alternative Measure Proposed by the Obama Administration

Through the corporate media there is gross misrepresentation involving the discussions over the budget cuts and possible changes in the formula which determine Social Security payment increases. The fact of the matter is that these measures are not necessarily related to the federal budget deficit. The Social Security system has a separate trust fund that has more than enough reserves to maintain payments to retirees, survivors and people living with disabilities.
The Consumer Price Index for Urban Wage Earners and Clerical Workers (CPI-W) is an instrument used to project the yearly cost of living adjustment (COLA) that is applied to beneficiaries. The idea behind this measure is to boost the annual inflation-adjusted increases in order for recipients to keep up with the constantly escalating prices of

housing, food, health care and other necessities of life in the U.S. CGPS in its study notes that "The Obama administration proposes to substitute the regular CPI-W for the chained Consumer Price Index for all Urban Workers (CPI-U), a measure of inflation that takes into account substitutions of less expensive goods when prices for other alternatives go up. This substitution would reduce the amount by which the COLA is increased annually—a reduction of about $3 for every $1,000 in benefits—and its effects would be compounded over time." Objectively this new measure could substantially reduce the purchasing power of those who have a greater reliance on Social Security and SSI payments. This instrument also fails to take into account the higher costs associated with health care services and prescription drugs.

Proposed Changes Will Further Impoverish African Americans

Statistics and studies issued by the Social Security Administration (SSA), the Joint Center for Economic and Political Studies (JCEPS) and the Center for Disease Control (CDC) indicate that 47 percent of African American seniors rely on Social Security for more than 90 percent of their retirement income. E percent of African American retirees are dependent upon Social Security as their sole household income. As recent as 2010, nearly 20 percent of African American adults over 65 had income levels that were below the federally-determined poverty line. This compares with 7 percent of non-Hispanic whites of the same age level.

Also as a result of life circumstances and inadequate access to healthcare, African Americans are more that require costs that are not covered through insurance programs. Moreover, the life expectancy for

Af l receiving of benefits. In addition, there is a higher rate of people living with disabilities among the African American population where the total number of people receiving benefits is nearly 20 percent Black, although African Americans only constitute 10 percent of the overall workforce. In regard to the impact on children, 21 percent of children receiving disability benefits are African American even though they are only 15 percent of the youth population. With specific reference to Medicaid, the Joint Center African American and Latino populations. The same research institute argues that these cuts would in companies since people would still need care whether it is funded by the government or not.

The report, **"Medicaid: A Lifeline for Blacks and Latinos with Serious Health Care Needs,"** *published by Families USA, "reveals that making cuts to Medicaid fails to reduce costs, instead it shifts the burden to states, families, hospitals and the uninsured. In fact, in some cases, the report notes, cutting assistance for treatment can actually increase costs over the long run."*

JCEPS continues pointing out that "As policymakers consider sharp cutbacks in the Medicaid program, this report brings an important potential consequence of their actions to the table – that cutting particular, those who depend on the program to manage and treat their chronic illnesses," said Ralph B. Everett, president and CEO of the Joint Center for Political and Economic Studies. (October 2011) T opposed by the trade union movement, the Congressional Black Caucus as well as civil and human rights organizations. An alliance of these forces with retiree groups could exert the necessary pressure to drop these draconian policy proposals and to put forward demands that enhance these programs that benefit the working class and the poor.

The federal budget deficit is the direct result of the failure of the U.S. government to tax the rich and to enact drastic cuts or eliminate the Pentagon budget. There must be a political movement to resist these actions which are making an attempt to reduce the deficit on the backs of the youth, senior citizens and the most marginalized segments of the working class and nationally oppressed." **By Abayomi Azikiwe Editor, Pan-African News Wire**

REAL SOLUTIONS

Those who are oppressed cannot look - in any way – to their oppressors to solve the problems of their oppression. To think the oppressors will end their vested interest in oppression is the epitome of unconsciousness and foolishness! Only the most naïve and /or those who are ignorant of U.S. foreign and domestic policy, or perhaps those who choose to turn their heads and shut their eyes and ears to reality would believe that the American government has ever - in the past, currently or will ever in the future - provide for the domestic tranquility of U.S. citizens. When the masses have benefited it was only by token and by accident – ***in the U.S., profits supersede healthcare!***

BROKEN PROMISES: *Education*

Obama said, pledged and promised, *"the best method for upward mobility and advancement is education"*; yet. his and the American racist ruling class record, relative to education, is a charade

An unquestionable response on the part of African people – particularly – in the U.S. was and is the cry for reparations on the part of the U.S. government. Notwithstanding, the romantic and narrow perspective of many Black people {particularly in the U.S}, the reparations movement is morally and historically justified. The unforgivable audacity and cultural sin of President Obama's total denial of reparations and his deaf ear to any reparations assertions shows his and the ruling class's depravity. *)(Obama Drama: A Strategy of Neo-Liberal Deception,* Obama countered the reparations argument with his assertion that the best thing for Africans in America and for the mass of working and poor people in America was to pursue education – according to Obama – *the best method for upward mobility and advancement*; yet. his and the American racist ruling class record, relative to education, is a charade and a transparency of broken promises and deception! *{See: (Hedges, 2011); The Phenomenon of Obama and the agenda for Education: Can hope audaciously trump neoliberalism? (Carr & Porfilio, 2011)(Obama Drama: A Strategy of Neo-Liberal Deception, by Gideon Odinga Mukhtar-Amazon.com}* One of Obama's biggest supporters, Professor of African American Studies and Religion at Princeton University, Cornel West, who took part in 65 campaign events for Obama, "now nurses, like many others who placed their faith in Obama, the anguish of the deceived, manipulated and betrayed"

PROMISES broken

- **Cut the growth of college tuition and fees in half over the next 10 years**
- He set a goal to lead the world in college graduates by 2020, and cut the growth of college tuition and fees in half over the next 10 years
- Proposed bringing together community colleges and businesses to train 2 million Americans for good jobs that actually exist now and are waiting to be filled."
- **Create 2 million more slots in our community colleges** so people can get job training.
- **Cut tuition increases in half over 10 years**.
- Recruit, Prepare, Retain, and Reward Teachers
- **Obama will also create Teacher Residency Programs** that will supply 30,000 exceptionally well-prepared recruits to high-need schools.
- **Address the Dropout Crisis**: Obama will address the dropout crisis by passing his legislation to provide funding to school districts to invest in intervention strategies in middle school - strategies such as personal academic plans, teaching teams, parent involvement, mentoring, intensive reading and math instruction, and extended learning time.
- **Address the Dropout Crisis**: Obama will address the dropout crisis by passing his legislation to provide funding to school districts to invest in intervention strategies in middle school - strategies such as personal academic plans, teaching teams, parent involvement, mentoring, intensive reading and math instruction, and extended learning time.

- **Expand High-Quality Afterschool Opportunities**: Obama will double funding for the main federal support for afterschool programs, the 21st Century Learning Centers program, to serve one million more children.
- **Expand Summer Learning Opportunities**: Obama's "STEP UP" plan addresses the achievement gap by supporting summer learning opportunities for disadvantaged children through partnerships between local schools and community organizations.
- **Support College Outreach Programs**: Obama supports outreach programs like GEAR UP, TRIO and Upward Bound to encourage more young people from low-income families to consider and prepare for college.
- **Reform for Kindergarten through High School**
- **Reform No Child Left Behind**: Obama will reform NCLB, which starts by funding the law.
- **Improve the assessments used to track student progress** to measure readiness for college and the workplace and improve student learning in a timely, individualized manner.
- **Make Math & Science Education a National Priority**: Obama will recruit math and science degree graduates to the teaching profession and will support efforts to help these teachers learn from professionals in the field. He will also work to ensure that all children have access to a strong science curriculum at all grade levels.

A promise is a sincere pledge to do what has been pledged. The value of a promise is based on the sincerity of the pledger and even more important, the ability of the pledger to carry out what was stated. With respect to the Obama administration, neither the sincerity nor the ability was ever present; moreover, the current history has made transparent the hypocrisy and the deception!

DRASTIC CUTS IN PUBLIC EDUCATION, BUT COFFERS OF THE RICH AND MILITARY SPENDING EXPAND EXPONENTIALLY

Along with the layoffs, other generalized cuts in public education and the prolific closer of schools across the country, are the attack on teacher salaries and benefits; it is crystal clear that education is not a priority by the U.S. government, despite executive promises. The indisputable facts bear out this reality are being wielded. Also included in this attack are increased out-of-pocket fees for health coverage. Recent contracts signed between the city and the Philadelphia Federation of Teachers (PFT), the largest union representing educators, have already undermined health care coverage.

States de-fund public education through expanded voucher schemes

State governments across the country are continuing the nationwide drive to dismantle public education through the expanded use of vouchers, "education savings accounts," and tax-credit scholarship program, diverting an ever-increasing amount of public money from the public education system to private schools. Currently, 17 states facilitate the funneling of public money to private schools through the use of such programs. In the 2011-2012 school years alone, $350 million that would have gone to public budgets instead paid for private scholarships of about 129,000 students. This allows for wealthy families to siphon money previously allocated for public schools, which they themselves were not using, to pay for the private education of their own children, while contributing nothing at all. In 2013, U.S. states cut higher education spending by nearly a third.

Wall Street turns *student loan debt into profits* while college and public education for the masses approaches catastrophe and inaccessibility

For the one in five Americans with student loan debt, it is a dreadful nightmare, but for Wall street and corporate predators, it is an investment opportunity. The anti-people sequester budget cuts, implemented by means of a pretentious crisis generated through the conspiracy of the Democrats and Republicans will hit low-income students by reducing Federal Work-Study and Supplemental Educational Opportunity grants by about $86 million. Loan fees will go up and student aid administration funds will be cut. Much of the financial aid already granted will be withdrawn, forcing students into additional loans. The fourth quarter 2012 statistics from the Federal Reserve Bank of New York Federal Reserve Bank of New York has shown that student debt has tripled over the last eight years. It found that 43 percent of 25-year-olds had student debt in 2012, an increase from 27 percent in 2004. Moreover, 35 percent of people under 30 who have student loans are at least 90 days late. For all student borrowers currently in the repayment process, nearly 30 percent are delinquent, giving student loans a higher delinquency rate than any other loans, including credit cards.

A report by the research group Demos indicated another aspect of the crisis revealing the debilitating effect of poor credit on job seekers. The report showed, not only are millions of people unable to pay their college loans, but because of their debt crisis, their ability to find work is severely impacted. The report revealed that 47% of employers conduct credit checks before hiring, according to the study. The decision to hire even for low-wage entry-level positions such as maintenance work, telephone tech support, delivery driving, supervising a stockroom or food service now routinely involves a credit check.

Over half of recent college graduates are either unemployed or underemployed. No wonder there are staggering levels of loan defaults. Of course, capitalism will always seek to make a profit off of the victims it has created. In the case of the student loan crisis, the enormous debt became a very lucrative profit! There is an enormous amount of money to be made money when there is $1 trillion worth of debt. Collection agent and debt seller, Sallie Mae (SLM) announced that it had sold $1.1 billion worth of new student loan debt securities. The publicly traded firm also noted there was a whopping 15 times more demand for the highest-risk, highest-return batch than there was supply. The *Wall Street Journal* commented that "boom times may be back for the student loan market!" There has been a decided uptick in the purchase of student loan securities. In 2012, SLM sold $13.8 billion worth of these bonds, making $514 million in the fourth quarter, a 12.5 percent increase over the previous year.

"The ultimate measure of a man is not where he stands in moments of comfort, but where he stands at times of challenge and controversy."
Dr. Marin L. King Jr.

The hypocrisies and betrayal of the Obama administration's broken promises, relative to education, are in reality, a result of a hidden hand. Deception is a criminal that travels in partnership with hypocrisy; the latter travels behind the former so as to conceal its' true intent! Despotic rule utilizes deceptions and seek to conceal hypocrisies to maintain and further its interest!

Chapter Five: State Sponsored Terror From Above and Below:

Pawns of Azazyel

I decided to refer to the term *"Azazel"* in this segment. The intent of this chapter is to highlight, warn and encourage understanding and resistance to the massive use of technology in the attaining and controlling of surveillance and military mechanisms of the growing American police state! Azazel is a term used in the Hebrew Bible and it describes a fallen angel or demon. Specifically, Azazel is represented in the <u>Book of Enoch</u> as one of the leaders of the rebellious Watchers – devil angels that fell with Lucifer - in the time preceding the flood. Azazel taught men sciences of destruction, the art of warfare, of making swords, knives, shields, and coats of war. Instead of using technique and knowledge for peace and social enhancement, Azazel represents, in short, the legacy of treachery of those who would cut deals with devils to advance in earthly power. U.S. State Sponsored Terror from above and below speaks to the use of military and spy technology in the domestic and foreign policy of a killer State such as the U.S.

It has been said that no lie can live forever, and the unearthing of buried truth regarding drone assassinations of children and many innocent along with the exposure of the nefarious ease dropping and electronic surveillance by the U.S. , both domestically and internationally, has made transparent the deceit, treachery and lies of despotism - so clear for all to see! Even the major system media must now give some time and lip service to a groundswell of protest and cries for investigation, exposure and rectification. A Washington Post editorial noted that "No government has ever relied so extensively on the secret killing of individuals to advance the nation's security goals." The New York Times described Obama's role as "without precedent in presidential history, of personally overseeing the shadow war. The record of American government terror is not short , nor is it new! These long-distance homicides and selective assassinations with Presidential approval, have been taking place secretly for at least 50 years. The only novelty in recent revelations about hit lists, and the use of drones, is the openness with which they are discussed – much of which is due to the actions of Mr. Edward Snowden!.

In a bone-chilling history of America's assassins in the aftermath of 50 years of massacres, selective assassinations committed by the U. S., the book, "*Assassination Nation*", by Doug Noble, gives vivid and substantiated proof, in three sections, of the horrid murder policy of the U.S. The first describes the lethal Phoenix program Vietnam, which he describes as the original source of terrorist strategies and tactics used later. The second part is about the well-known kill lists of people in Latin America and those less publicized, targeting individuals on other continents. The third section addresses the resurrection of the Phoenix program in Iraq and Afghanistan, as well as in a growing number of countries with which the U.S. is technically not at war. Developed in

CIA AND DRONES METHODS & NUMBERS

Since 2009{12 years} the U.S. has employed drone warfare not only in Iraq, Afghanistan, Pakistan, Africa, and it would be an unforgivable error if we did not include the *drone surveillance terror of the NSA, FBI and Homeland Security!* Drone warfare is unique and a method of choice in the technologically advanced armies of oppression. The pilot from thousands of miles away uses a joystick to steers the drone and, when deemed appropriate, fires the missiles or takes the surveillance photo. This kind of manhunt involves executions without arrests, without trials, without hearings and without verdicts and for sure without pity or mercy even on children, innocent, defenseless and non-combatants!

A report by the London-based Bureau of Investigative Journalism (BIJ) has found that the U.S. Central Intelligence Agency deliberately attacked rescue workers and funeral processions in follow-up strikes after drone missile attacks on insurgents in Pakistan's tribal areas. The findings were made public on the group's web site. According to the organization, which includes British and Pakistani journalists, at least **50 civilians were killed in follow-up** strikes while they were attempting to help victims of an initial CIA drone attack. Dozens more were killed by

Overall, the group found that between 2009 and 2012 **between 282 and 535 civilians** have been credibly reported as killed, including more than 60 children. Pakistani officials and humanitarian aid workers have reported much higher figures for the death toll in Pakistan's tribal areas, as many as several thousand. *The current death number by Feb. of 2014 U.S. has probably killed more innocent people through drone strikes than the 2,606 U.S. citizens killed on 9/11. Although there are no hard numbers for the public to source, the statistical ratio from leaked sources can provide reasonable assurances that, at some point in the last year, we have surpassed this threshold.* In timing follow-up strikes so they incinerate people who come to the aid of victims of an initial blast, the CIA has employed a tactic that U.S. officials regularly denounced as "terrorism" when carried out by insurgents during the Iraq and Viet Nam wars. Such attacks are carried out as a deliberate effort to inflict maximum casualties on the civilian population. Experts on international law have characterized these follow-up drone missile strikes as war crimes. Clive Stafford Smith, who has fought for the release of many innocent men held in Guantanamo Bay, told BIJ the drone strikes "are like attacking the Red Cross on the battlefield. It's not legitimate to attack anyone who is not a combatant."

The Obama administration was stung by the BIJ report. It came only days after Obama said, in a much-publicized comment in a forum on YouTube, that "drones have not caused a huge number of civilian casualties." He called the strikes "a targeted, focused effort at people who are on a list of active terrorists." A senior American counterterrorism official charging that those who brought to light the reality of U.S. mass murder in Pakistan were "elements who would like nothing more than to malign these efforts and help Al Qaeda succeed." Such a bold face red neck lie flies in the face of the recent revelations of the U.S.s in bed strategy with the Al Nursa Front in Libya and with the reactionary forces of Al Quada Iraq. The U.S. does not lie some of the time; it lies all of the time!

STATS IN U.S. DRONE TERROR

Total reported killed: **2,383 - 3,019**
Civilians reported killed: **464 - 815**
Children reported killed: **175**
Total reported injured: **1,149-1,241**
Total strikes: **312**

- The U.S. claims the drones are a vital tool that have helped them almost wipe out the leadership of al Qaeda in Pakistan. But others point out they have stoked enormous anti-American sentiment in a country with an arsenal of 200 nuclear weapons.
- Peter Singer, director of *the 21ˢᵗ Century Initiative* at the Brookings Institution, points out the operation has never been debated in Congress which has to approve sending US forces to war.
- **So dramatic is the switch to unmanned war that he says the U.S. now has 7,000 drones operating and 12,000 more on the ground,** while not a single new manned combat aircraft is under research or development at any western aerospace company.
- After a remarkable lack of debate, there is starting to be unease in the U.S. at the lack of transparency and accountability in the use of drones particularly as the campaign has expanded to hit targets in Libya, Yemen and Somalia and until recently to patrol the skies in Iraq.
- Three U.S. citizens were killed by missiles fired from drones in Yemen last September. Anwar al Awlaqi, an alleged al Qaeda operative, was deliberately targeted in what some have described as the US government's first ever execution of one of its own citizens without trial. His colleague and fellow citizen Samir Khan also died in the attack. Two weeks later Awlaqi's 16 year old son Abdulrahman died in a strike on alleged al Qaeda militants.*{ without arrests, without trials, without hearings and without verdicts and for sure without pity or mercy even on children, innocent, defenseless and*

non-combatants!}
- **T**he fact that the operations are carried out by the CIA rather than the U.S. military enables the administration to evade questions. The Agency press office responds to media inquiries on the subject with no comment and refusal to give names of those killed or who are on the target list.

Reported deaths and injuries

- Pakistan 2004–2013

CIA Drone Strikes
- Total strikes: **381**

Obama strikes: **330**

Total killed: **2,537-3,646**

Civilians killed: **416-951**

Children killed: **168-200**

Injured: **1,128-1,557**

- Yemen 2002–2013

US Covert Action
- Confirmed drone strikes: **59-69**
- Total killed: **287-423**

Civilians killed: **24-71**

Children killed: **6**

Injured: **74-185**
- Possible extra drone strikes: **85-104**
- Total killed: **300-481**

Civilians killed: **23-46**

Children killed: **6-8**

Injured: **79-107**
- Other covert operations: **12-77**
- Total killed: **144-377**

Civilians killed: **59-88**

Children killed: **24-26**

Injured: **22-115**

- Somalia 2007–2013

US Covert Action

- Drone strikes: 4-**10**
- Total killed: **9-30**

Civilians killed: **0-16**

Children killed: **0**

Injured: **2-24**

- Other covert operations: **8-15**
- Total killed: **48-150**

Civilians killed: **7-42**

Children killed: **1-3**

Injured: **13**

DRONES: TOOL OF A GROWING POLICE STATE

Terror Scare, The NSA Exposed,

"FAA Modernization and Reform Act of 2012"

White House Press Secretary Jay Carney in responding to questions from reporters continued the White House's line of lies and deception by his refusal to offer any evidence to corroborate the American government's claims of the necessity of drone warfare as a response to U.S. Armed forces and NSA-Homeland Security terror threats. However, not a single piece of concrete evidence has been produced to back up the government's assertions that U.S facilities abroad and perhaps within the U'S. face an imminent threat of attack by Al Qaeda-linked forces. Notwithstanding the indisputable revelation that the U.S. finances and arms the Al Nursa Front and Al Qaeda-Iraq. The substance of the supposed threat likewise remains completely vague, with government sources admitting they have no information on a specific target or time of attack. The use of fear and scare tactics has been a favorite tool of dictatorship!

A long series of U.S. terror scares since the September 11, 2001 attack has become a well-worn pattern in America. Officials of the executive branch issue vague and threatening alerts. Congressional leaders, after closed-door briefings by the intelligence agencies, repeat the warnings. The system media enlarges the alarm uncritically, seeking to panic the public into unquestionable and visionless support of the government. Such alarm shouting takes place admits a disquieting silence and unconscious apathy among the American citizenry in general. Not a single voice is raised to question the claims or essential premises of the panic campaign. In an earlier book, _Chickens Come Home to Roost: A Critical Analysis of American Capitalism in Crisis_ , I am emphatic on the issues of deception as a police State strategy; moreover, such subterfuge is a means of mass distraction to the red-hot issues and realities of an empire in disarray and plummeting to destruction:

p.9. "I was not confused. **_9-11 was the American attack on America._** It was an event that was created in part to pave the way for a police state of repression. It was a horror in which the U.S. government and Zionist intrigue cooperated for mutual benefit. It allowed the ruling classes in America and Israel to avoid an internal political and economic crisis. It was the excuse the America ruling class needed to pave the way for invasions of numerous sovereignties; if not by direct intervention, then by way of allowing this to occur and /or encouraging it to take place. **BUT WHY?** Just being conscious of the history of America made it crystal clear to me that the American ruling class, the executive administration at the time, a significant part of the armed forces, the varied intelligence networks and many government officials had a hand in this somehow, some way. It was done out of desperation and very much related to the internal and external capitalist crisis that was swiftly growing in 2001, a crisis brought on by the very nature of the beast that is today called world imperialism, American capitalism, and American government. The proof of this was one of the driving forces to write this book." The timing of these latest panic measures comes after months of nonstop revelations about massive U.S. government spying on the American people, including the collection of both metadata and the content of the telephone conversations and e-mail of virtually every person in the United States.

The U.S. media has played its traditional reprehensible role, in reinforcing reports of the government's claims as both promote an atmosphere of anxiety.   This design of conspiracy, cover up and deception can be traced back to the 1993 bombing of the World Trade Center, in fact, it can be traced back to The Sinking of the battleship Maine, 1898 – leading to the Spanish-American war *{Chickens Come Home to Roost: A Critical Analysis of American Capitalism in Crisis}* In the 1993 bombing of the World Trade Center a former Egyptian army officer, Emad Salem ***acting as a paid FBI informant***, had actually participated in building the bomb, claiming that the original plan had been to substitute harmless powder for the explosives.***{Paul DeRienzo's interview with William Kunstler about the role of Emad Salem in the World Trade Center bombing trial. Broadcast on WBAI Aug. 3, 1993}*** One only wonders, were the Boston bombings the result of such an operation that got out of control? Or did sections of the state know about it and it was allowed to go forward? Like the Benghazi affair, much evidence points o a massive government cover up! How the Boston Marathon bombing plot unfolded and what motives lay behind it are still not known. Only one thing is certain: whatever the source of this terrorist atrocity, it will be used by the U.S. government for its own advantage. The aim is once again to utilize the tragic events to justify the massive buildup of the government's military, security and intelligence apparatus. The immediate response to the attacks has been a security clampdown not only in Boston, but nationwide, to condition the public for another expansion of the militarization of American society. The events in Boston have laid bare the modus operandi for the establishment of dictatorial forms of rule in the US. One or another violent act carried out by disoriented or disaffected individuals, perhaps with the help of elements within the state, is declared a terrorist event. A state of siege is imposed suspending democratic rights and establishing military-police control.

Such strategies of desperation and anxiety reflects the near panic of the American racist ruling class and corporate-financial elite in the face of escalating social discontent, intensified by extreme nervousness over the perilous state of global finance capital. What haunts the ruling class is not the fear of a terrorist attack, but the trepidation of a new financial collapse, with the likely consequence of massive social upheavals, rebellion and revolution! When the richest 5 percent of the population controls over 60 percent of the wealth, what else can one expect. *{Who Rules America, by G. William Domhoff}*

Another fundamental cause of the crisis of in America is the negative eruption and corruption of U. militarism. The power of the military/intelligence apparatus has grown immensely, particularly since the end of the Soviet Union, as the American ruling class has turned to military aggression as a means of offsetting the decline in its global economic position. *{The Military Industrial Complex at 50 by David Christopher Naylor Swanson}* The professional military, segregated from society at large and antagonistic to it, has acquired ever-greater influence over political affairs and civilian authority. As always, imperialist war is irreconcilable with genuine people's power and democracy.

American liberalism as a distinct political tendency has ceased to exist. The lining up of the Democratic Party behind the "war on terror," and the external aggression and internal repression carried out in its name, has made clear that there is no section of the ruling elite that will defend democratic rights. The Obama administration, and more significantly, racist ruling class which controls it, has expanded the right-wing, antidemocratic policies of the Bush administration, and is without question the most reactionary in U.S. history. And as always, the filthiest role is played by the media and its leading personnel. From day one, they turned the airwaves into a continual rumor mill, making one unsubstantiated claim after another in an effort to sow fear and panic and justify the police-state measures being taken. As CNN anchor Chris Cuomo, son of the former Democratic governor of New York and brother of the state's current governor, told viewers, "We've only been showing the feeds that authorities are comfortable with." *For more than a decade, the so-called war on terror has been used as the overarching pretext for the erection of the infrastructure of a police state.*

The NSA Exposed -Thank you, Mr. Snowden

The Snowden issue demonstrates – once again – that the snake is poisoned by its own venom. Moreover, the NSA's trampling on people's rights is indication of a far more ominous beast. Many criticize the NSA - its invasion of privacy and surveillance of almost every facet of people's lives, as an affront to the 4th amendment to the U.S. Constitution, which in essence speaks to the right of the people to be secure in their persons, houses, papers and effects, against unreasonable searches and seizures, and no warrants shall be issue, but upon probable cause, etc. No doubt, the NSA is an insult to justice and a violation of people's inalienable rights. However, if we must speak of indisputable rights being negated, then, we must also say the U.S. Constitution is immoral and an affront to the inalienable rights of the Indigenous people of the western hemisphere. Looking at it in these broader and more *"just"* parameters, one must conclude that of course the NSA is a people's violation, for it is an appendage of an unjust government and political economy; a product of the irreconcilability of class antagonisms!

HISTORY OF NSA

The National Security Agency (NSA) is the central producer and manager of signals intelligence for the United States. Estimated to be the largest of U.S. intelligence organizations in terms of personnel and budget, the NSA operates under the jurisdiction of the Department of Defense and reports to the Director of National Intelligence. The NSA is primarily tasked with global monitoring, collection, decoding, translation and analysis of information and data for foreign intelligence and counterintelligence purposes.

The awareness of the horror, mass control and mass surveillance of the fascist state of Germany has shocked and appalled millions. However, what is disquieting in relation to this realization is the apparent blindness of the same fascist procedures being used in the U.S. today and the "unconscious" apathy within the general population of doing nothing about it. It has been said that the limits of tyrants are prescribed by the endurance of those whom they oppress. In Germany, too many waited too long to speak out. Too many were too late, too weak and did too little*! Totalitarian States and despotism thrive on apathy, unconsciousness and lack of mass organization!*

COMPARISON: Nazi Germany and the Nazification of America

The victims of Americanism who reside in America - *American citizens* - would benefit themselves greatly by studying German fascism and the Nazi police State. The likenesses of U.S. despotism and the totalitarianism of Germany under Hitler are frighteningly similar; the results of not being conscious of this will lead to victimization geometrically worse than the horrors of Nazi concentration camps and ovens!

The German police State was characterized by: comprehensive surveillance of the population, all criticism of government and descent were considered treasonous, fear and intimidation were ubiquitous, mass unconsciousness and lack of organization was predominant, business and profit interest were dominant over the social welfare, the militarization of society, major media - especially news and entertainment – were supportive of the State, most elected leaders danced to the tune of the government and business sector, *civil-rights spokespersons were - for the most part – instruments of the State used to detour social activity away from violence and to insure any descent was non-threating to government and business*! For many of the German people, the Nazis developed a policy of intimidation. Fear became a by-word for those who did not support Hitler. The wrong comment overheard by a Nazi official could have very serious consequences. This was the situation for nearly 17 million people. A large and visible police force was required to keep this sizeable group under observation and control. Police brutality was rampant under the Gestapo. The police were allowed to arrest people on suspicion that they were about to do wrong. This gave the police huge powers. Just think of the amount of harm and tyrannical devastation the German State could do if it had access to the technology that America now has.

The American police State is tremendously more sinister and threating than Hitler's Germany ever was!

Nine Signs That America Is Rapidly Becoming Worse Than Nazi Germany

1. Nazi Germany was a totalitarian Big Brother police state that monitored everything that German citizens did.

2. / In Nazi Germany, authorities could stop you and search you at any time and for any reason.

3. Once the Nazis took power, they rapidly implemented gun control legislation and later on they took all of the guns away from the populace.

4. Under Nazi Germany, society became very highly militarized.

5. In Nazi Germany, the prisons were absolutely packed.

6. Under Adolf Hitler, paranoia was standard operating procedure.

7. In Nazi Germany, big corporations thrived but workers' rights and benefits deteriorated.

8. In Nazi Germany, the church and religion was controlled by the fascist State.

9. In Nazi Germany, the oppression of the African was most severe. Racism was intensified. We were the last hired and the first fired, and by law, Blacks, were ordered to be sterilized. *{See: Hitler's Black Victims: The Historical Experiences of European Blacks, Africans and African Americans During the Nazi Era by Clarence Lusana Clarence ; Also:*

Germany's Black Holocaust, 1890-1945: The Untold Truth!, by Firpo W. Carr }

FAA Modernization and Reform Act of 2012

Ominous Implications

> *The conversion of a welfare state to a police state is the result of militarized imperialism abroad and the ascendancy of finance capital at home, as well as the proliferation of security state agencies and related private industries and the strategic role of rightwing Zionists in top positions of the police state apparatus.*
>
> *{The Great Transformation: From the Welfare State to the Imperial Police State*, by James Petras}

As the rights of millions diminish with each drastic offensive of the increasing American police State, the ominous implications of the FAA Modernization and Reform Act of 2012 is a clear sign of worst to come! A little-noted amendment to a $63 billion Federal Aviation Authority appropriations bill indicates definite trouble ahead for millions. President Barack Obama signed the bill, the "FAA Modernization and Reform Act of 2012", into law in February 14 year. The bill clears the way for an enormous expansion of the use of Unmanned Aerial Vehicles (UAVs), commonly known as drones, over U.S. territory.

The technology of Unmanned Aerial Vehicles (UAVs) and the ideology that produced it is a brutal appendage of the explosive growth of U.S. militarism abroad and the steady advance of police state repression domestically. UAVs and even more sinister technology have become infamous the world over as instruments of U.S. military aggression and assassination in the *"global war on terror"*. Their use has expanded exponentially over the last decade. In 2001, the U.S. military arsenal included barely 50 drones. Now, it has a fleet of some 7,500, ranging from small Raven drones, used for surveillance, to the better known Predators and Reapers, capable of hovering unseen over human targets for up to 28 hours and firing Hellfire missiles with devastating effect. During the Obama administration, the drone strikes have dramatically escalated, and have claimed nearly 3,000 victims since 2004, the great majority of them unarmed men, women and children

These massacres and assassinations are carried out by remote control, with CIA and military operatives targeting their victims on computer screens from cubicles in the Nevada desert and offices near Langley, Virginia. Now (UAVs) will be a standard weapon of police departments and NSA, and who knows who else or what else! The legislation signed by Obama requires the FAA to expedite the process through which government agencies are able to secure permission to operate their own drones over U.S, soil. The FAA will be establishing a pilot program to integrate drones into the "national airspace system" in six test areas around the country. By 2020 an estimated 30,000 drones could be operating in U.S. skies—including military, police and corporate-owned UAVs. They are already in use by the Department of Homeland Security in monitoring U.S. borders.

Association for Unmanned Vehicle Systems International Extension of the Military Industrial Complex

A key driving force behind the legislation was the Association for Unmanned Vehicle Systems International, whose members include such giants of the military-industrial complex as Lockheed Martin, Boeing, General Dynamics, Northrop Grumman and Raytheon, and whose lobbyists reportedly wrote the language of the bill. The market for drones already approaches $6 billion annually and is expected to double over the next ten years. This proliferation of drones sets the stage for a vast expansion of state spying upon American citizens. Drones can carry sophisticated surveillance equipment capable of not only photographing and video-recording every step taken by individuals once they leave their homes, but also intercepting electronic communications and cellphone calls and they can be programed to kill!.

"Drones give the government and other (UAV) operators a powerful new surveillance tool to gather extensive and intrusive data on Americans' movements and activities," {*Jennifer Lynch, staff attorney for the Electronic Freedom Foundation*}

Given what we now know - thanks to Mr. Edward Snowden - , the U.S. wars in Iraq, Afghanistan, Pakistan, Somalia and the sordid history of U.S. wars and invasions, there is no reason to believe that drones inside the United States will not be armed, putting to use within the United States the experience the U.S. government has obtained from its killing campaigns abroad and the assassination of U.S. citizen, Awlaki. In this regard, it is worth recalling the arguments used to justify the passage of the National Defense Authorization Act signed into law by Obama. With this bill, the U.S. Congress enshrined in law the president's extra-constitutional power to condemn anyone, including U.S. citizens grabbed on American soil, to indefinite military detention without judicial review, and without trial, kill them!

The rationale offered by congressional backers for this escalating Police State is that the *"global war on terror"* has turned the entire planet into a battlefield, including the U.S. itself. There is no reason why a government that accepts this reactionary claim would shrink from using drones to kill people within the United States, while it uses them regularly for assassination abroad. With the backing of the Obama administration, both the Republican and Democratic Parties and with barely a word of disapproval from within the media or the political establishment as a whole, the machinery is being put in place for a full-blown American military-police state.

In conjunction with this process of technological warfare is the unprecedented social polarization between the financial aristocracy that monopolizes wealth and power and the masses of the people, a polarization that will inevitably give rise to resistance, rebellion, organization and a mass demand for fundamental system change! The racist ruling elite is much aware of the inevitable and is turning to the same bloody and ruthless methods it has used to advance its interests abroad!

In, "*Assassination Nation*", Doug Noble, irrefutably shows that long-distance homicides and selective assassinations with ruling class and consequently, presidential consent, have been going on clandestinely for at least 50 years. The only difference is that now there are more publicized revelations and public scrutiny about hit lists and assassinations with the use of drones. "Those who are mortified by the latest revelations of Obama's hit lists have much to learn from a more comprehensive, historical perspective on US killing around the globe," says Noble, who divides the analysis of half a century of the of massacres and targeted killings by the USA into three sections:

- Section 1 describes the lethal history of the US Phoenix Program in Vietnam, the original source of subsequent US counter-terrorist tactics and strategies.
- Section 2 revisits briefly the well-known history of US kill lists and assassinations in Latin American countries, followed by the somewhat less-well-known history of US kill lists and assassinations in countries on other continents.

Section 3 traces the resurrection of Phoenix in Iraq and Afghanistan, and in a growing number of "countries we are not at war with." The US Phoenix program was a highly secret operation applied in 1967 by the CIA in Vietnam aimed at "neutralizing" the "Vietcong" infrastructure. This meant assassinating South Vietnamese civilians suspected of supporting North Vietnamese or "Vietcong" fighters. The Phoenix operations killed over 20,000 people between 1967 and 1972. The My Lai massacre, hardly an isolated incident, was itself a Phoenix operation. With abundant data and arguments, Doug Noble describes the repercussions of this program in Latin America. An even more revealing report of CIA atrocities can be found in, "*The Secret Wars Of The CIA, Americas Third World War*", by John Stockwell

Chapter Six BEYOND U.S. IMPERIALISM AND OBAMA DRAMA

"OUR FREEDOM LIES IN A STRONG AFRICA AND COMMUNITY POWER."

"That only a Revolutionary mass, Pan African Socialist Party can achieve true African unification is an objective fact not a subjective wish by the Osagyefo. A cursory glance at Africans' centuries - long struggle with its rich and diversified experiences and thanks to Osagyefo's work, insures the fulfillment of this prerequisite for total liberation. The struggle for a unified, socialist Africa has been raging though undetected by many. This demand by the masses will soon gush forth the hurricane, which has built up since the "winds of change" of the 50's. Osagyefo's vision will be inevitable reality. No force on earth can stop Africa. She will be totally liberated, unified and socialist."

Osagyefo's Vision, by Kwame Ture

In his book, <u>Neo-Colonialism the Last Stage of Imperialism</u>, Kwame Nkrumah makes it clear that one of the last battle grounds for imperialism will be in Africa, where imperialism will find its inevitable death! He also says, {"A determined attack must be made on the entrenched position of the minority reactionary elements amongst our own peoples. For the dramatic exposure in recent years of the nature and extent of the class struggle in Africa, through the succession of reactionary military coups and the outbreak of civil wars, particularly in West and Central Africa, has demonstrated the unity between the interests of neocolonialism and the indigenous bourgeoisie." *Class Struggle in Africa }* The US strategy for Africa and its use of reactionary puppets in domestic and foreign policy is doomed to failure; this is not only true for Africa but , Iraq, Lebanon, Afghanistan, Columbia, the us and wherever the voucher of US imperialism and Zionism chooses to fly or roost! Yes! Capitalism, Zionism and imperialism have caused the underdevelopment of Africa but the rise of African to world dominance and influence will and must assuredly lead to the decline and foreseeable death of imperialism **AND THANK GOD AND GOOD RIDENCE!**

"I referred to some of Obama's ideas which point to his role in a system that denies every principle of justice. Some throw their hands up in horror if anything is said to criticize the important personality, even if it is done with decency and respect. This is usually accompanied by subtle and not so subtle darts from those with the means to throw and transform them into the elements of media terror imposed on the peoples to sustain the unsustainable."

REFLECTIONS BY COMRADE FIDEL
CONTRADICTIONS BETWEEN OBAMA'S POLITICS AND ETHICS

This fourth and final chapter will speak to suggested solutions and alternatives to the Obama Drama - in other words - if not capitalism, if not US neo-liberalism and neo-colonialism, if not oppression then what? Marcus Garvey said that when all else fails, "conditions will make us organize"!

"I AGREE WITH NKRUMAH,

PAN-AFRICANISM IS THE SOLUTION TO THE PROBLEMS OF PEOPLE OF AFRICA DESCENT." From Malcolm X Speaks

"We shall measure our progress by the improvement in the health of our people; by the number of children in school, and by the quality of their education; by the availability of water and electricity in our towns and villages, and by the happiness which our people take in being able to manage their own affairs. The welfare of our people is our chief pride, and it is by this that my Government will ask to be judged."

Dr. Kwame Nkrumah, "Broadcast to the Nation," 24, December 1957

In past chapters, I have tried to show the real meaning of the strategy of deception that is contained in the orchestrated frenzy of the Obama campaign, the election of Barack Obama, the Obama administration, the policies mouth by Obama and the domestic and foreign policy of the US in its' current phase of neo-liberalism and empire decline. ***Constructive criticism must at least attempt to offer corrective actions and solutions, and revolutionary consciousness demands such***. Consequently, this fourth and final chapter will speak to suggested solutions and alternatives to the Obama Drama - in other words - if not capitalism, if not US neo-liberalism and neo-colonialism, if not oppression then what? Marcus Garvey said that when all else fails, "conditions will make us organize"! **Organize or perish!** In the short and long run, the only solution to the political-social and economic problems of African people lies with the context of the African Revolution! Revolution is a social-political phenomenon that proceeds in a dialectical pattern, that is to say ***conscious organized quantity must be built and made to lead to conscious organized quality.*** Revolutionary struggle is a process that does not move in a straight line; it is not an event but a series of strategic stages and stages of transition with varying modes of struggle moving through periods of reform, turbulence, "apparent" stagnation, rapid movement, flows and ebbs and always much struggle. The Worldwide African Revolution is certainly no exception to the laws of development. It is critical to know what to do under a given set of circumstances and how to best move the historical dynamic forward. An imperative in this regards is ideology - "correct ideology" - , strategy, organization, cadre development and mass development- leadership and involvement! Action without thought is blind and thought without action is empty!

BRIEF "Bullet" SUMMARIES OF CHAPTERS ONE, TWO AND THREE

The following are very brief summaries - by way of bullet points - of the first three chapters, which are crucial in an understanding of this final essay which seeks to offer some ideas towards an alternative and solution

Chapter One- Obama Drama: Neo-Colonial Deception & Intrigue

*"Neo-colonialism is essentially a strategy of deception. In the Obama case, capitalism (finance capital) and White racist ruling class power- by way of the US government - , gives the false impression of Black control, Black Power or real people power. In reality, finance capital maintains control – politically and economically – and also controls the strings of a puppet leadership that give a semblance and lip service to democratic concerns and populist interest, but in reality it is the same old " **oppression as usual!"***

* ❖ Obama's unquestionable political allegiance to his ideological and financial sponsors argues in a tenaciously and culturally embarrassing way for a person that has betrayed his people, prostituted his ethics, and as Franz Fanon points out in, "Pitfalls of National Consciousness" *{Franz Fanon, The Wretched of the Earth}*, shows Obama to be a willing instrument of his people's own oppression
* ❖ Obama is nothing more than the mouth piece for a forked tongue domestic and foreign policy and a deceptive mask that will seek to trick many in Africa, the African community and the world into accepting U.S. strategy, U.S. military, U.S. intrigue, U.S. capitalism and U.S. neo-colonialism. How can you be for the little person and at the same time tenaciously being for the oppressors of the people?
* ❖ If politics makes strange bed fellows, then Obama has amassed a curious assemble of sleep around partner- particularly morally filthy Zionist bed fellows.
Obama is merely the product of a right wing and heavily influenced Zionist grooming process and effective marketing campaign which has utilized media savvy and technology to sell this new version of a very old product - the Democratic Party "friend of the people," - previously disgustingly

incarnated in the "insurgent" candidacy of Jimmy Carter in 1976, then in the "man from Hope," Bill Clinton himself, in 1992 and now, the misleading smiling face of Obama.

❖ Although many Africans – especially those in the U.S. – "went crazy" for Obama, most voted and supported him based on emotions and aspirations of change. Whereas I understand the emotions and the aspirations, Obama's aspirations are not the aspirations of his people.

❖ The financial backers and major promoters of the Obama presidential campaign and the Obama presidency are some of the most racist right wing elements in the world.

❖ *OBAMA IS A STRETGY OF NEO-LIBERAL AND NEO-COLONIAL DECEPTION!*

Chapter Two: The Domestic Strategy of American neo-liberal Ruling class (The Class Struggle)

Ø "Class struggle is a fundamental theme of recorded history. In every non-socialist society there are two main categories of class, the ruling class or classes, and the subject class or classes. The ruling class possesses and controls the major instruments of economic production and distribution, and the means of establishing its political domination, {including the US presidency} while the subject class serves the interests of the ruling class, and is politically, economically and socially dominated by it. There is conflict between the ruling class and the exploited class. The nature and cause of the conflict is influenced by the development of productive forces. That is, in any given class formation, whether it be feudalism, capitalism, or any other type of society, the institutions and ideas associated with it arise from the level of productive forces and the mode of production. The moment private ownership of the means of production appears, and capitalists start exploiting workers the capitalists become a bourgeois class, the exploited workers a working class. For in the final analysis, a class is nothing more than the sum total of individuals bound together by certain interests who as a class they try to preserve and protect." *{Kwame Nkrumah, Class Struggle in Africa}*

- ❖ The U.S. presidency has always been a mass deception. American capitalism and imperialism is controlled by those who own and control the major means of production. Those who think that one man or a president controls the U.S, economy and government are fooled as much as a child believing in an Easter bunny and a White- or Black Santa clause coming down the chimney. *{See: Who Rules America: by G. William Domhoff; Also see: The Rich and the Super-Rich: A Study in the Power of Money Today: by Ferdinand Lundberg.}*
- ❖ **Obama condemned reparations**
- ❖ Obama's cabinet is a roll call of Zionist and supporters of the illegitimate and immoral government of Israel
- ❖ One cannot be pro-Israel and pro Black at the same time. The two are in total contradiction
- ❖ Obama condemned the world conference on racism.
- ❖ Obama has supported most of the Bush foreign policy

Chapter three: US Foreign policy and neo-liberalism- The Africa strategy

- ❖ The global reach of the United States is backed by its' foreign policy by which the United States interacts with foreign nations. U.S. foreign policy from 1776 to present, in general - and specifically in relation to Africa - has been a policy and strategy of invasions, destabilizations, assassinations, State sponsored terror, deception, orchestrated coup de tau, (media, NGO and organizational manipulation), resource pillage, oppression, exploitation, murder, underdevelopment, terror and a forked tong diplomacy, backed by a gun boat-air assault and infantry perverse persuasion, " currently financed by an over 13 trillion dollar economy and the new mouth of U.S. imperialism, **Obama** , a puppet that is seeking to increase the military budget as he calls for billions more to bail out the super-rich!

❖ The foreign policy of the U.S., in this beginning of a new presidency in 2009, will only follow the path of the treacherous legacy that birthed this country, a tale of genocidal assault on the indigenous of the Western hemisphere, the oppressive utilization of Asian labor, the exploitation of White workers, and the enslavement of the African. **YOU CAN NOT BE A GOOD PRESIDENT OF AN EVIL EMPIRE!**

Africa's and Africans relationship with Europe, and more specifically the United States, has always been one of contrast, contention and conflict of cultures. For the most part, this relation has been one of people's sovereignty vs. conquest, profiteering and exploration vs. cautious suspicion and repulsion and African humanism vs. categorical anti-humanist predation on the part of empire-quest mentality and ideology of capitalism and U.S. imperialism! *{Walter Rodney, How Europe Underdeveloped}*

❖ Not only was Africa the birth place of humankind, but the natural resources and the people of Africa have been vital for all empires and is certainly vital for the empire ambitions of US capitalism. This point has been stated throughout the book. ***We have already made the point of the strategic importance of Africa with regards to oil, but oil is only one of the vital natural resources within the bosom of the continent of Africa.*** Oil is only one of the life sustaining mineral resources that lie in the womb of mother Africa and oil is only one of the resources that can be used in a **"strategic political-military sense," for the liberation of Africa and humanity!**

❖ "Africa accounts for a significant proportion of U.S. imports-100% of industrial diamonds; 58% of uranium;48% of cocoa; 44% of manganese used in producing steel, 40% of antimony to harden metals; 39% of platinum, 36% of cobalt for jet engines and high strength alloys, 33% of petroleum, 30% of beryl used in weapons and nuclear reactors, 23% of chromite used in gun barrels, 21 % columbium-tantalum for heat resisting alloys in missiles and rockets and 21% of coffee," from Imperialism and Dependency Obstacles to African Development by Daniel A. Offiong.

SO WHAT IS THE ALTERNATIVE AND COURSE OF POSITIVE ACTION?

We stand on the shoulders of the giants that came before us. In my view, much of the solutions to our current problems are in the ideologies, efforts, legacies, experiences and strategies of our {African} glorious history. In making these suggestions of an alternative and solutions, <u>I am not so foolish as to offer them as my ideas</u>. Perhaps my wording and expressions, but certainly not my ideas. I am indebted to the **"masse of the people- especially the courageous African masses"** <u>the people are the genuine makers of history</u> and in particular, I am indebted to the ideology of Nkrumahism-Tourism, the great Revolutionary Pan-Africanists, and my years of experience and learning while in the All African People Revolutionary Party (AAPRP) and the current AAPRP-GC (GC meaning HQ in Guinea Conakry). **{PLEASE NOTE THAT I DO NOT CLAIM TO SPEAK OFFICIALLY FOR THE AAPRP-GC, AS THIS WRITING REFLECTS MY INDIVIDUAL VIEWS!}**

"OUR FREEDOM LIES IN A STRONG AFRICA

AND COMMUNITY POWER ."

"I began revolution with 82 men. If I had to do it again, I'd do it with 10 or 15 and absolute faith. It does not matter how small you are, if you have faith and plan of action."

"As a revolutionary, I am a force of nature"

Fidel Castro

"To contemplate the building of community power in the US, organizational development and a revolutionary struggle not in isolation of the world struggle – and for African people particularly, the world wide Africa struggle, would be more than myopic, it would be disastrous and downright stupid!" Gideon Odinga Mukhtar

At this time (2014) when U.S. imperialism is playing its **{Black Ace card}** internationally and domestically, the U.S. also is in a pre-revolutionary crisis. A pre-revolutionary crisis period and stage is where the oppressed are in a situation where the oppressor (the enemy) has overwhelming control. This is known as a zone under enemy control. ; yet in this state of affairs - due to the increasing oppression, growing police state, deteriorating political—economic-social conditions of the people along with the people's growing distrust and disappointment with the government - the potential for mass unrest and resistance is a time bomb with a very short fuse! An excellent example of this stage is the current condition of the African in America and Europe and many places in the world where our people are. The definition of this phase highlights much of the immediate tasks that the people, revolutionaries and progressive reformers must address in their day to day struggle and work, especially within the strategic context of building a Revolutionary Pan-African struggle. It is within the major organization work and tasks of this phase that the initial and ongoing contacts and relationships are made for the building of an international coordinate struggle. One clear example of this was the international travels that Malcolm X was making during the latter part of his life{ 1963 to 1965 } and the contacts that his organizational efforts were making with African revolutionary leaders in African and the building of a relationship with revolutionary China and Cuba. We can also look at the domestic and international activities of the Black Panther Party, the Black Panther Party for Self-Defense, the Revolutionary Action Movement and the All African People's Revolutionary Party and of course the national liberation struggles and movements of Africa, Latin America, the Caribbean and Asia.

To contemplate the building of community power in the U.S., organizational development and a revolutionary struggle in isolation of the world struggle – and for African people particularly, the world wide Africa struggle, would be more than myopic, it would be disastrous and downright stupid! With such understanding and review of the strategies and mistakes of the organizations and struggles just mentioned are many lessons and models for building a movement, organization building and networking and meaningful and mass empowering community development and without doubt for the making of people's revolution.

During this phase { pre-revolutionary crisis period } , and within the context of progressive reformist and especially revolutionary organizations, there is must be emphasis on careful buildup of political, social, and economic organizations. Mass consciousness, vanguard and mass organization building work, community influence, institution building, community control and self-reliance are major concerns during this phase. <u>The accomplishments of this current phase within the U.S. is crucial for the next phase the revolutionary crisis.</u>

In this phase because of **objective and subjective conditions** a change has taken place in the power and control situations in a country. The oppressor power - as a result of the systemic contradictions of **capitalism** - is in a situation of crisis and desperation. Because of the oppressive conditions and the growing resistance to oppression the government does not have the strong hold on society as it did in an enemy held situation. **In terms of objective conditions**, there is much instability within the economic structure, financial institutions and the country is characterized by political-economic instability. For example, America today is rapidly approaching this situation, in spite of the fact that there is yet much disorganization and lack of consciousness among the oppressed, particularly the African and Latino oppressed.

Many of the **objective conditions** for revolution exist in America. This is characterized by the intense oppression of the people, high unemployment, drastic health conditions, poor housing, repression on political organizations, rising prison populations, poor education, economic crisis, massive downsizing, rising discontent and resentment towards the government, intensification of class struggle among the oppress, increased racism, increased gender oppression, increased corruption within the government, disunity among the oppressive ruling class, division within the armies of the ruling classes, defeat in military operations of the government, mayhem of capitalist production, intense competitive price wars being waged among all the major sectors of the American corporate industry, massive layoffs, less investment and fierce competition among investors, comprehensive business failures and bankruptcies, fewer jobs, less consumption and even less reason for business to invest, increased and intense criminalization of the youth, student dissent on a massive –national scale, massive anti-war protest and demonstrations, social misery and health conditions become epidemic, rise in radicalism and people resistance, comprehensive distrust of government, massive and nationally destabilizing protests and demonstrations, lack of confidence in government and elected officials, system destabilize strikes, consumer alarm and growing panic, rise in crime rate- poverty breeds crime, rise in inflation and impending depression, increase trade deficit and trade wars, government and economic policy based on desperation, the rise of a police state and fascism, the reliance on repression and police terror replacing the ability to control and mislead by way of distraction(*media-brainwashing, sports and entertainment distraction, drugs and mis-education, family destabilization and strategies to encourage and induce fear.*) The oppressor relies more and more on brute force to maintain control. In this situation, it becomes clearer every day that the government and economy is crumbling and unable to meet even basis needs of the people! These objective conditions mentioned are the things that revolutionary crises is made of. As you are aware many of these conditions already exist in America in 2005. It will only get geometrically worse in 2010 and on towards the fall of the American government and collapse of its' political-economic system!

The length of each phase depends on the changes between the enemy forces and peoples, and also on the changes in the international situation and its relation to positive organizational forces within the people's struggle. ***This is why the demand of mass consciousness and organization along with building international relations and alliances are crucial in this and all phases.***

Currently the necessary primary subjective conditions within the struggle of the masses do not yet exist amongst the people. In the US - among Africans and Latinos masses for example - the subjective conditions of wide spread cultural, nationalistic, anti-government and revolutionary consciousness is very weak and for the most part does not exist in any mass-organized manner. Yet, oppression can breed resistance ad consciousness. **This reality indicates some of the immediate tasks of this period.** In specific terms, the subjective conditions must be the programmatic actions of revolutionaries – *particularly in the pre-revolutionary and revolutionary crisis phases* – by this we mean: mass consciousness, working unity between organizations, community institution building, effective and politically consolidated coalitions and united fronts, significant numbers of the people in organization - particularly revolutionary organizations, the initial and further development of mass revolutionary political parties and "preparation and development" of the people's revolutionary armies. Although these vital subjective factors do not currently exist within the context of the struggle with the U.S. – **to the degree that they must be built** - history does give proof that such factors do and will develop! ***The objectives conditions help provide the needed subjective factors, and the development of the subjective factors take advantage of the objective conditions.*** The successful accomplishments of the tasks of this phase are the essential material conditions that provide for making

<u>an enemy held zone become a contested zone.</u> Consequently, some of the requirement during the pre-revolutionary crisis phases are:

➢ Identification and development of a conscious core of revolutionaries and cadre development and strategic placement within the mass experience and struggle.

➢ Development of a conscious core and placement of the conscious core with the sectors of the people when and where mass resistance and struggle is at its highest point of positive action.

➢ Institution building in terms of organization and neighborhood/community power bases Programmatic interaction and networking among African organizations- leading up to building of an African united front.

➢ Development of Revolutionary Pan-African relationships and alliances with world revolutionary, socialist, anti-imperialist and progressive forces.

➢ Mass positive action

➢ Building of militant independent party and an all-African Revolutionary Pan-African political party

➢ **Development of Revolutionary Pan-African relationships and alliances with world revolutionary, socialist, anti-imperialist and progressive forces.**

Within these eight areas are the basis for the alternative to U.S. neo-liberal policies and its current and very deceptive - **Black Ace card strategy - the feeble and essentially weak** *"puppet Obama"*
.

Practice without thought is empty; thought without practice is blind. History is the movement of the dialectic – the continuous movement of positive and negative forces; and of course the hand of GOD is omnipresence and always behind the scene. *We act the way we think, and for conscious action, there must be a social-political basis of thought guiding it partly arising from the mass of reality and in tune affecting it.* It can be convincingly argued that matter is primary, but ideas are critical to guide the direction in which matter will develop. The need for a conscious, highly skilled force of organizers is a vital perquisite for social alterations, social reform, social movements and revolution. This conscious core must be guided by correct ideology and strategy and dedicated to the purpose. Then their strategic placement and/or involvement in the segment of the people where the dialectic for forward movement and change is most dynamic are required. This core of the conscious can serve as a catalyst, spark and mass inspired vanguard force; it cannot be a vanguard in any elitist or Marxist sense; <u>in other words this writer highlights a rejection of the view that the people cannot make their own history. The internal dynamic is the basis for change!</u>

Thousands of cadre cells or circles must be developed. They must be organized throughout the people in as many sectors of the people as possible. This is a tactical issue of identifying the pulse of the people's response to oppression and their pro-active struggle for betterment and assessing the degree, and form of engaging struggle, using the situation to ameliorate a problem while at the same time advancing the dialectic forward- organizing around the peoples attempts and aspirations to rid themselves of oppression and exploitation while building the revolutionary struggle towards more organize and mass endeavors. This is a matter of mass development or strategic involvement within the mass and organizing. These nuclei of conscious organizers must be made to exist throughout the organism of the mass of the people. Even though the core organizers may not be able to immediately implement much of the revolutionary theory they are learning, they must study ad discuss it nevertheless and engage in the struggle for development as part of the mass. Consequently revolutionaries must find themselves involved in reformist work to advance it towards revolution! "Dialectics inform us that when the negative dominates, the positive is reform it becomes an obsolete on the road to freedom; it must give way to revolution." "The reforms mention in the book will not avoid revolution; rather, rather they will help advance the African revolution and consequently the world socialist revolution." "Integration was a subterfuge for the maintenance of White power. Africans in the Democratic party represent powerlessness visibility." {*See: Black Power, The Politics of Liberation: Stokely Carmichael and Charles Hamilton*}

In my spiritual/conscious view, the quotes above implies that ultimately, oppress people can only look to GOD and themselves regarding the ending of their oppression. Most certainly the oppress cannot look to their oppressor nor their oppressors solutions. One of the essential aspirations and demands of the genuine: Black Power, Africa nationalist and developing Revolutionary Pan-African movement of the sixties was the reverberating insistence for cultural integrity and self-sufficiency; ***the right of African people to be independent of western and colonial thought, to define our own reality, our own intentions and our own destiny!***

This enlighten path towards development stands unconditionally in opposition to integration or any assimilationist policy. It is not about trying to prove ourselves to America nor is it about trying to be all that America expects, but to focus - primarily – on our cultural development and power to insure that we are in continuous control of our development - a development that is not in the interest of American capitalism. A prerequisite for this is institution building in terms of organization and neighborhood/community power bases.

THE SEARCH FOR NEW FORMS

It is imperative to build bases of power in the community by way of organizational cooperation and collective efforts and by doing so turn our community into a base of power. We must strive to at least have much more political influence moving towards control of our schools in our communities, the hospitals, stores, spiritual centers, colonial agencies and executive, judicial and legislative arms of the colonial machine. We must strive to at least have much more political influence moving towards control of the executive, legislative and judicial arms of the colonial machine and make it move in our interest or make it weak, dysfunctional or non-effective. We must gain and expand control of the colony or make it uncontrollable by the enemy.

Around the world, African people are over two billion strong. While it is utterly romantic to think that all African people can be united into a force for liberation and good, it is quite feasible and in fact essential that a quality mass force { including millions of people } can be developed in the interest of Africa people. We must build an international and coordinated force for Africa and African people's development and cultural self-sufficiency. Political relationships with revolutionary Africa and with African revolutionary forces of African people in the Diaspora must be built. Alliance with the progressive forces of the world must be built. Relationships of cooperation and strategic planning must e built with the socialist and anti-imperialist forces of the world. AN isolationist strategy has no place in the liberation efforts of African people. Every community organization needs to have an agenda that includes aspects of this need for relationship building. **TO MAKE THIS EFFECTIVE THE AFRICAN MUST BE WITHIN STRONG ORGANIZATION!**

Positive action must overwhelm negative action and this must manifest in mass involvement in organization, mass consciousness rising, and significant increase in the interaction and programmatic relationships among African organizations. Unity must not just be a slogan but a reality. Africans must be in organization and African organizations must be about a coordinated strategy leading toward very broad organizational coalitions, formations for development and liberation and genuine African united fronts and Revolutionary Pan-African coordination and organization. Such a strategy should even envision the organizational relationship with the indigenous and Latino forces of positive action. With regards to African people, this must take place wherever African people are. My experience and research has informed me that this fact must be emphasized on the continent and in the Diaspora but it is particularly in the Diasporic areas of the U.S. that this point must be emphasized the most. Particularly because of this point, I have added this *Special Note to Africans in America* and also because it appears that nowhere is the Obama deception more prevalent than in the U.S. among Africans who have been the victims of racist-capitalist Americanism!

Special Note to African in America

Careful analysis of this strategy and how it relates to the Revolutionary Pan-African movement and the vanguard position of the African in the developing revolutionary struggle in the Diaspora of the U.S. and western hemisphere is, particularly for Africans and other people of color, an effective strategy to defeat imperialism. The African and the oppressed people of color in the western hemisphere have a crucial role in the Revolutionary Pan-African and socialist movements leading to the defeat of U.S. led world imperialism. In coordination with the struggle in Africa, a combined African – Latino/people of color strategy - can bring about a decisive blow to the U.S. and is essential to the destabilization, defeat and overthrow of the U.S. government. The U.S. has long tried to prevent such an alliance and is well aware of its revolutionary potential in not only the U.S. but throughout Latin America. A closer analysis of this potential leads to a strategy for revolutionary victory in Latin America and the U.S.

No one knows capitalism like the African! We know it from the rape, exploitation and penetration of Mother Africa up to the current oppression and exploitation of the African neighborhoods and communities of the Africa world of today. The African has unfortunately been an integral part of American capitalism. We have labored and died to build it. In fact, it has been built on the backs of the African. As soon as we **GET UP AND STAND UP FOR OUR RIGHTS AND DIGITY**, capitalism will come tumbling down. As soon as the African in America, throughout the Diaspora and in Africa start acting in a truly self-reliant and independent manner, the American capitalist system and government is disaster-prone!

The resistance of Africans to capitalism has never totally abated and will not stop until we organize and fight our way to our total and just liberation. African people are moving towards freedom and no power on earth can stop us. In spite of the devastation of capitalism, the Revolutionary Pan-African movement marches forward. As a result of the racist-capitalist slave commerce, African people are scattered and suffering in many parts of the world. ***Revolutionary Pan-Africanism is the correct strategy and objective for genuine African freedom!, the core of the Black revolution is in Africa, and until Africa is free the, the black man (women) lacks a national home. Africans of the world must be cognizant of our political responsibilities, no matter where we are in the world!***

All Africans - no matter where they are in the world - have a responsibility to join or create organization wherever they are. By way of people's mass organization and revolutionary parties, the struggles of Africans in all parts of the world must recognize the necessity to control the African community, zone or African country where they reside in , while at the same time helping to build a coordinated struggle - **worldwide** - between Africa communities and countries, realizing Africa is the core. ***<u>Of course even this is relative and interdependent with the advances and successes of the Africam Revolution on African soil!</u>*** Consequently, the - worldwide - African revolutionary struggle can be divided into zones or hemispheres of struggle. North America, for example, must be seen as a zone of the African Revolution - ***as a matter of strategy, moral principle and historical truth***! <u>It cannot be viewed as a liberation struggle that is separate and not an integral part of the African Revolution</u>. Africans in America cannot view themselves as a different or "new" type of African. Yes, our experiences in America - in a sense - are new and in that sense, unique, but the struggles of Africans in other parts of the Diaspora is also "new" and unique. That does not make Africans in one part of the Diaspora a different people. The advances of the liberation struggle in one area is really meaningless without the liberation of Africans as a whole. No African is free unless the masses of Africans everywhere are free, and again, the core of any Africa struggle has been and will always take shape around the continent of Africa. The African revolution must be seen as one struggle with a variety of unique situations based on geography and historical experiences, for sure, but basically, the struggle of African people has an overall unity of history and oppression. Our response to that oppression has always been basically in common. The African revolution is one, with **one goal, one aim and one destiny!**

Such a strategic view demands responsibilities for Africans in each strategic zone. With respect to North America, there is a tremendous amount of work to be done. For sure, Africans in America are the most technologically advanced mass of Africans in the world. We Africans in America live in one of the most crucial and strategic nerve centers of U.S. led imperialism. (Of course not losing sight of the fact that the **"most crucial nerve center for imperialism"** is the neo-colonial hold on Africa). Africans in America have more exposure to resources, technical equipment and information than Africans in any other part of the world; they are captives behind enemy lines with enormous potential to give support to the Mother land and to neutralize, disrupt, destabilize and destroy vital political, economic and military capitalist infrastructure, yet, considering all this potential and accessibility, the African in America is one of the most politically backward, unorganized and unconscious Africans than anywhere in the world. This is pathetically horrendous and culturally irresponsible. I hate to say this about us Africans in North America, but it is true. Such a "hard line" and bitter assessment is not new; it was said over forty years ago by a person that no responsible African would dare to challenge, Big Red! The Revolutionary Pan-Africanist Malcolm X was just as critical about Africans in America. His acid criticism was contained in his immortal speech, "Message to the Grass Roots", where he gave a class analysis in speaking of the house Negro and the field Negro.

A closer look at the strategy of U.S. imperialism to prevent capitalist destabilization and a seizure of power inside of the U.S. and Latin America shows how fundamental a coordinated assault by way of the defeat of neo-colonialism in Africa can set the U.S. up for a frontal attack within the confines of the U.S. Also the positive reaction on the part of the revolutionary movement of Africans and Latino in America and throughout the Western hemisphere reveals the power and potential anti-capitalist threat of an combined African-Latino-Western indigenous resiliency for revolutionary production and is a pointer to the inevitable conquest of good over evil and positive action over negative reaction within the geo-political context of the United snakes! **This must not be underestimated by those who seek the overthrown of the American capitalist system and the corrupt government and armed forces that seek to maintain its existence.**

The building of a militant independent party and/or an all-African Revolutionary Pan-African political party is essential "OUR VICTORY IS INEVITABLE FOR GOD IS ON OUR SIDE. THE ONLY QUESTION IS WHAT ROLW WILL YOU, WILL YOR ORGANIZATION PLAY IN THIS INEVITABLE REALITY." Minister Gideon odinga mukhtar
gideonodinga@gmail.com